# Homeowners Association and You

## *The Ultimate Guide to Harmonious Community Living*

Marlene M. Coleman, MD
Judge William Huss

SPHINX® PUBLISHING
AN IMPRINT OF SOURCEBOOKS, INC.®
NAPERVILLE, ILLINOIS
www.SphinxLegal.com

Copyright © 2006 by Marlene M. Coleman and William Huss
Cover and internal design © 2006 by Sourcebooks, Inc.®

All rights reserved. No part of this book may be reproduced in any form or by any electronic or mechanical means including information storage and retrieval systems—except in the case of brief quotations embodied in critical articles or reviews—without permission in writing from its publisher, Sourcebooks, Inc. Purchasers of the book are granted license to use the forms contained herein for their own personal use. No claim of copyright is made to any government form reproduced herein. All brand names and product names used in this book are trademarks, registered trademarks, or trade names of their respective holders. Sourcebooks and the colophon are registered trademarks of Sourcebooks, Inc.

First Edition: 2006

Published by: **Sphinx® Publishing, An Imprint of Sourcebooks, Inc.®**

Naperville Office
P.O. Box 4410
Naperville, Illinois  60567-4410
630-961-3900
Fax: 630-961-2168
www.sourcebooks.com
www.SphinxLegal.com

This publication is designed to provide accurate and authoritative information in regard to the subject matter covered. It is sold with the understanding that the publisher is not engaged in rendering legal, accounting, or other professional service. If legal advice or other expert assistance is required, the services of a competent professional person should be sought.

*From a Declaration of Principles Jointly Adopted by a Committee of the American Bar Association and a Committee of Publishers and Associations*

**This product is not a substitute for legal advice.**

*Disclaimer required by Texas statutes.*

**Library of Congress Cataloging-in-Publication Data**
Coleman, Marlene.
  Homeowners association and you : the ultimate guide to harmonious community living / by Marlene M. Coleman and William Huss. -- 1st ed.
    p. cm.
  Includes index.
  ISBN-13: 978-1-57248-551-8 (pbk. : alk. paper)
  ISBN-10: 1-57248-551-5 (pbk. : alk. paper)
  1. Homeowners' associations--Law and legislation--United States--Popular works. 2. Homeowners' associations--United States--Popular works. I. Huss, William H. II. Title.

KF576.Z9C65 2006
643'.2--dc22
                                                          2006011558

Printed and bound in the United States of America.
SB — 10 9 8 7 6 5 4 3 2 1

To all fair-minded owners, Board members, and managers of Community Associations everywhere.

# ACKNOWLEDGMENTS

Writing a book is always a collaboration—but in this case, there were two different types of collaborations going on simultaneously. We were writing the book together while also gaining as much knowledge as possible from everyone we came in contact with who is involved in Community Associations.

Our greatest appreciation is extended to Karen Conlon, the president of CACM (California Association of Community Managers). Karen's vision for what the manager/homeowners association relationship can be remains vivid and growing. She was an excellent resource to us and provided great support.

Leslie Kossoff—an executive advisor and friend—provided invaluable assistance and support in our understanding of how organizations can and should be run. Her effort on behalf of this book is reflected in making the management process easier to understand for any association to pursue. Without her, this book would not have been written.

Our very special thanks go to our former editor, Dianne Wheeler, who recognized our passion for the subject and made it possible to put it in print, and our current editor, Michael Bowen. It is a pleasure and an honor to be associated with this fine house.

Special thanks go to Judy Kleinberg, an author herself, for her insightful contributions to our vision of Community Association living—not only what it is, but also what it can be.

Finally, our appreciation is extended to CAI (Community Associations Institute) and CACM and their instructors—as well as to all the managers, homeowners, and experts who were so generous in sharing their knowledge and experience with us.

# CONTENTS

## Part 3: Managing the Community

# INTRODUCTION

Homeowners Association and You is designed as an information resource and a practical guide for solving problems regarding Associations. The book is presented in three parts. The first part addresses how the Community and its Association are structured. The second part provides an overview of the legal issues the Association confronts and what to do about them. The third part addresses how the Community is managed and the part you can play—whether as a knowledgeable resident, Committee member, or Board member—in improving its operation and success.

The chapters are laid out by major topic areas—those that everyone must know something about. Within the chapters, each subject area is discussed in detail with questionnaires, checklists, and forms provided. The appendices provide you with additional resources and information to assist you as you go forward.

## EVALUATING THE COMMUNITY

The questionnaires and checklists are evaluation and improvement tools for determining the state of your Community and your Association. They can and should be used more than once. That way, you can track your progress based on the point at which you started.

Even more, the questionnaires and checklists will provide you with the opportunity to develop a vision for your Community. No matter where you live or in what type of Community, each resident has a picture of how that Community should look, feel, and operate. The evaluations allow you to determine how you are progressing toward that vision, where there are opportunities for improvement, and what actions should be taken so that the vision can and does become reality.

As you read through the book, you may want to gather a group of other residents to join you in completing some of the evaluations. If you are a member of the Board, you may want to arrange a special session to discuss the evaluations and the Board's vision for the Community.

You may decide to get alternative views from non-Board or Committee members—in effect, the silent majority of residents—about how they see the Community and its operations. Think of it as an informal focus group. Marketing companies do it all the time to make sure that they are on the right track. Why not use a tried and true technique for getting as much input as possible?

The main thing in using the questionnaires and checklists is to be as honest and objective as possible. It is very rare that everything is perfect or perfectly awful. Most situations are a combination of what you want and what you are surprised to find—for the good and the bad. So when you use the evaluations, use them one at a time, take your time in answering them, and consider the answers carefully before you decide to take action.

## TRACKING AND MONITORING PROGRESS

Some of the actions you need to take might be addressed in the forms that appear throughout the book. The forms are tracking and monitoring tools to ensure that the details of the Association and its business are being adequately overseen.

In some Communities, the use of these forms may be the first time any of these issues or projects are formally tracked or monitored. Do not worry—there are no wrong answers. You just need to keep track of what is going on so that before you move on to the next issue or project, you make sure the ones in progress are moving in the right direction, in the time frames and at the costs you expected.

The forms are designed to show progress, as well as expected and desired outcomes. They are tools for management, Committees, and the Board to use to make sure that what is going on is what should be going on. Most of these forms can be displayed in the management office. Many of them should be incorporated into the Board records.

The questionnaires, checklists, or forms are positive tools designed to help your Association and your Community. The more you work together with the other residents, the more successful you will be—individually and as a group—in achieving your Community goals.

## HOW NOT TO USE THIS BOOK

There are only a couple of pitfalls that you may find in using this book.

The first pitfall is when a resident would prefer to use the questionnaires, checklists, and forms as weapons rather than as tools. Unfortunately, there may be loose cannon residents—those Committee and Board members who try to use any type of evaluation as a means of pointing fingers instead of working to better the Community. If you find yourself or any of your Community members unconsciously going in that direction, stop the discussion and remind yourself and everyone else that everyone is on the same side. You are all working for the betterment of your Community and its Association. You are all working toward the same goals of survival and success—better living conditions, increased property values, greater safety, and the like.

The second pitfall occurs if you try to take on the whole content of the book all at once. A Community Association is a business—and a complex one at that. While everything ultimately needs attention, it is unrealistic to think that you can take on everything at the same time and be wholly successful. Do not try to do everything all at once. It will be overwhelming.

Instead, go back to why you first decided to open this book. What is the issue or problem you have questions about? What is its priority in the scheme of things? Is it a big issue or problem, or is it one that can be put on the back burner for a while?

Ultimately, Homeowners Association and You will get you to the answers you require. Prioritize the issues you plan on undertaking. Always look at the Community and the Association as a business. That way, even though you are dealing with your home, you can take a more objective stance, keep things in perspective, and simply work on each issue one at a time until you have them all taken care of. Eventually, you—and that vision for your Community—will be a guiding force and an attainable goal for you and the other residents.

HARMONY

It is not the absence of:
differences,
emotions,
and
conflicts.

It is the presence of:
respect,
kindness,
and
communication.

© Bill Huss 2003

# –1–
# COMMUNITY LIVING

The decision to purchase and live in a Community setting is different from any other residential purchasing decision you can make. From the moment you buy your residence, you become the co-owner of a business. The business you co-own is the business of your Community. The name of the business is your Community Association or Homeowners Association.

A Community Association is sometimes called a Common Interest Development (CID). Community Associations or CIDs can be one of four types: condominium, stock cooperative, community apartment project, or planned development. It is in your best interest to understand which specific type your Community is, since your rights and responsibilities as a homeowner can be affected.

Community living provides opportunities most home buyers cannot afford on their own. Whether it is access to a swimming pool and tennis courts or just having someone else handle the gardening, living in a Community setting provides a comfortable living experience.

However, Community living comes with responsibilities that apartment dwellers and single-family homeowners do not face. As a part owner of a business, you have a responsibility for more than just your own home. You also have a responsibility to help the Community be everything it can be—in safety, aesthetics, and financial value.

Fulfilling that responsibility is not difficult, but it does require an understanding of how the Community works and of how best you can be a contributing member to its success.

# BECOMING A PART OF THE COMMUNITY

Being a part of a Community means that you have to do more than live in your home. You have to become an active and interested part of the larger Community and its issues. This does not mean that you are required to serve on the Board or Committees. Not everyone wants to do that—and no one should be forced to hold such a position if he or she does not want to.

It does mean, however, that you should make sure that you know what is going on in your Community. After all, it is in your best interests to be informed. Ultimately, some of the decisions being made could have an impact on your property value or the safety of your Community.

Consciously or not, you have a vision for your home and your Community. That vision probably includes everything from how you will decorate the interior to the maintenance and care of the outside grounds and shared areas. You probably also think about the safety of your Community—how well it is lit inside and out, whether there is some form of a neighborhood watch program, and whether your Association is in contact with the local police department.

This is your home. You want it to be the best it can be, both inside and out. To make that happen and ensure that it stays that way, think about how things are done now and how they might be done better. You may not know the answers to some of your questions or complaints, but you do know that they deserve attention.

By being part of the Community—an active and vocal part—you bring your concerns to the attention of your friends and neighbors. What started out as a question or a private complaint suddenly has an audience. You may even find that there are others in the Community who share your thoughts and concerns, but have never voiced them before. By voicing your question or complaint, you open the doors for others to support and build upon your thoughts and ideas.

What makes Communities great is when the people who live in the Community and who share in its ultimate outcomes speak to how they can improve their Community. By doing so, you address what needs to be done for the Community from within and by others from outside.

Communities, when they work, build support within themselves. Everyone living within the Community knows that they are a part of a greater whole. It is not just their concern for their own home—it is a matter of what is best for the entire Community, both aesthetically and operationally.

Whether it is a question of new roofs, widened walkways, necessary plumbing updates, or whether the Association should hire a professional manager, as a member of the Community you must participate to make sure that your voice is heard. The only way you can be heard is if you speak. It may not be comfortable at first, but the outcomes more than justify the discomfort.

Not only will your voice be heard, but it will be incorporated into the larger whole of the Community to make yours and everyone else's living situation the best it can be. From there, it is easy to continue along that path and make every aspect of the Community better over time.

## Understanding the Business of the Community

You need to understand that the Community is a business. When you buy into the Community, you are also buying into the business of the Community. The business is represented and managed through the offices of the Community Association.

One of the common phrases in literature about Communities is that their Associations exist "to protect, preserve, and enhance" the Community. That is all well and good, but what does it really mean? It means that, in being the business end of the Community, the Association exists to look at and manage the needs of the Community objectively and with an eye toward its future. Without the Association, all the good ideas, questions, and complaints of the Community dwellers would go nowhere. With a well-run Association, a Community not only identifies, but acts and builds upon, the ideas and needs of its residents.

One of the best ways to understand the Association and its relationship to the Community is to understand that, as a business, it is actually separate and apart from the Community. This allows the business to remain objective. It also puts the responsibility on the residents who work within the Association—on the Board, in Committees, and as members—to understand that when they are working on behalf of the Association, they are not residents—they are businesspeople.

Businesspeople are different from residents. Businesspeople do not look at the needs of the individual—they look at the greater good. They see the business as a growing entity that must be safe and protected. They see the services the business provides as a way of satisfying the residents and making the Community the best possible place to live.

That is why the phrase "to protect, preserve, and enhance" makes sense. The business of the Association is to make sure that the property and living conditions of all the Community members remain in as good, if not better, condition than when they moved in. You want your home and your investment to be safe. The responsibility of the Association is to make sure that is the case.

As a member of the Community, you are also a member of the Community Association. This makes you a part of the business of the Community. Smart businesses are forward- and future-thinking. They are proactive and preventive. They think about what needs to be done, and then they make sure the actions that need to be taken are taken. When those actions are taken, they make sure the costs are contained, value is received, timelines are kept, and the outcomes of those actions are preserved and maintained.

Being an active member of the Community Association means that you need to understand how the business of the Community runs—how your Association works, what it is responsible for, how the Community legally and financially supports itself, and so on. You must also be committed to making the Community the best that it can be.

This may mean that you decide to become an active member of the Board or one of the Committees. It may mean that you begin attending Board or other meetings to make sure that your voice is heard.

However you decide to participate, remember that the Association exists for the protection of your home and investment.

The Association is not an enemy—nor is it particularly on your side. The Association is committed to the betterment of the Community and the property it oversees.

## Pride of Ownership

A very interesting phenomenon that occurs among people who buy in Community settings is an unconscious belittling of their living situation. People do not speak of their homes, they speak of their condos or townhomes. Somehow, they feel it is important to differentiate their homes from other people's homes. It is as if their decision to live in a Community somehow makes their living accommodations less than in single family homes.

After all, you do not hear people who live in single family homes referring to their properties as such. You never hear of a person saying that he or she is going home to his or her single family home.

However, Community residents have so much more. They own their own homes. They are able to choose to live in preferred areas because the prices are far more affordable than for single family residences. They have amenities—like swimming pools, tennis courts, and even garden areas—that are not always available to their single family home brethren. Also, they have conveniences—like being able to leave without worrying about the same level of break-ins as in single family residences—that they would not otherwise have.

People who live in Communities have more than neighborhoods—they have real neighbors. This is not just because they share walls. It is because they live in close enough proximity to one another to be able to converse. They meet each other in the hallways and by the garages. They see each other, along with their families, at the pools and in the gardens. They become familiar enough with each others' faces to know who belongs as well as who does not.

People who live in single family homes do not have those same opportunities. Move into a new neighborhood and see how long it takes before the neighbors begin to introduce themselves.

In a Community setting, there are both business and social opportunities to meet other Community dwellers. Whether in Board or Committee meetings, or by attending the various social functions that occur, residents quickly have the opportunity to become neighbors. As a member of a Community, you belong. This belonging should be viewed with pride. It also comes with a sense of responsibility to make the most of your Community for you and for the others who share it with you.

## BEING ACTIVE IN YOUR COMMUNITY

The best thing you can do for yourself and your Community is to become an active part of your Community. Think back to why you decided to live where you do. If you are just thinking about buying into a Community, think about why you prefer that Community over the others that you considered. What is it about the Community that makes it a good place to live? What will make it even better?

By being an active part of the Community, you are protecting, preserving, and enhancing your home, your property, and your investment. You are maintaining and improving your life and lifestyle. You are actively contributing to a better life for yourself, your family, and your neighbors.

You are not alone in your desire for a better Community. By becoming an active member of the Community and its Association, you will have the opportunity to share with others in your joint vision for your Community. You will be able to look at your home and say, *This is such a great place to live because I helped to make it that way*. Nothing could be better.

# –2–
# UNDERSTANDING THE STRUCTURE OF THE ASSOCIATION

As a co-owner of the Community Association, you have legal, financial, and managerial responsibilities—even if you do not perform those services yourself. In effect, you delegate the tasks of the Association to members of the Board, Committees, and management, who oversee and protect your investment. However, that does not mean you can just sit back and trust that your best interests will always be addressed.

Like any other business ownership, membership in a Community Association means you have to take an active part in the business of your Community. You need to know how it is doing financially. You need to know that it is protected legally, and whether there are any potential or pending legal threats to your Community. You need to make sure that the Community is protecting itself through adequate insurance and risk prevention procedures.

You also need to make sure that the management of the Community makes sense. Of all the challenges you will face, this is probably the most daunting and most frustrating. It is only when you start looking at the management of your Community Association that the human element appears. These are not only your representatives to the Community Association. They are your neighbors.

This human element puts additional stress on the management of the Association. The people who are holding the representative positions are doing so because they believe that they have something to offer. They give their time and their thoughts to better their Community—for themselves and for their neighbors.

For those not serving on the Board or Committees, it is easy to use the decisions being made and the people making them as target practice. Unless each person is knowledgeable about the issues being discussed and decided by the Board and Committees, it is both unfair and counterproductive for the other residents to simply take shots at the decisions and decision-makers.

Instead, each resident must take the opportunity to become knowledgeable about the business of the Community. How is it doing? How does the Association operate? What challenges are being faced? How have such challenges been handled in the past? How are decisions made and by whom? What are the checks and balances for the Community and its management and operations?

These are just a sample of the types of questions you should ask as you begin to evaluate your Community, its Association, and how the business is being run. Throughout this and the other chapters, you will be provided with guidance regarding the questions you should be asking, the answers you should be looking for, and the actions you should be taking.

## UNDERSTANDING THE ASSOCIATION

It is all well and good to say that you are a business owner and that the name of the business is the Community Association, but what does that mean? What is a Community Association? What do you have to understand about the Association so that you can play a positive role in its management and operation?

In its most simplistic form, the Association is the structure that supports the business needs of the Community. The operation of the Association is controlled by all of the governing documents, including but not limited to, the *Community Plan*; *Declaration, Covenants, Conditions, and Restrictions* (CC&Rs); *Articles of Incorporation* or *Association*; *Bylaws*; and, the *Rules and Regulations*.

The Association is a legal entity that continues to exist no matter who lives in the Community or how often the residences change hands. The Association provides continuity and protection to the Community, no matter how long you live there. For long-time residents, the Association provides a sense of protection. The responsibilities are known, so no matter who serves on the Board or Committees, the Association is designed to protect the residents' investment and living environment.

For shorter-term and new residents, the Association provides a sense of structure, rules, and regulations. This is particularly applicable for the common areas—those areas of the Community that are shared by everybody. By determining what is common and providing an overall protection of the Community, the Association both places limitations on and opens up opportunities for Community development, property enhancement, and increased property values.

While all Community Associations perform basically the same functions and services, each is different. No two can be exactly alike, because each Community, its residents, and its needs are different. No matter where you live or how large or small your Community, there are similarities in the basic duties and responsibilities of the Association.

Depending upon the materials you read, the duties and responsibilities of the Community Association will range from being all things to all people to being very few things to a very limited group of people. However, in its simplest, most straightforward form, you will find that there are four basic duties of the Community Association:

1. to ensure the repair and maintenance of the common areas;
2. to establish and collect assessments to pay the common expenses;
3. to ensure adequate reserves for future replacement of major components of the property; and,
4. to administer the rules and regulations of the Association.

If the Community Association successfully performs these duties, your investment is protected and you live in an enjoyable environment.

## Repair and Maintenance of the Common Areas

The Association exists, in part, to make sure that the Community is well maintained. That means walkways are clear and pavement is repaired when necessary; plumbing and other internal systems are maintained, and preventive maintenance systems are in place and implemented; elevators are checked regularly; trees are trimmed and grass is cut; roofs are checked, repaired, or replaced; and, the property is painted regularly.

The Association is responsible for making sure that all common areas are known and understood to be common. No one person owns the common areas. Everyone does—under the auspices of the Association. As such, the Association must take care of its investment and make sure that the property for which it is responsible is well maintained.

This is not an easy job. On any property there are so many common functions that the Association must have means to first identify what is common, then develop a repair and maintenance system to ensure that everything is in working order.

Individual residents often choose to interpret *common* as anything they do not want to deal with. Conversely, other residents will decide that what is common is actually theirs, and will be tempted to take actions that work against the Community's rules and regulations. Some examples of these different interpretations illustrate the problems faced.

**EXAMPLE:** A resident knew the Association was going to be painting the exteriors of all the buildings in the Community. However, when he found out that they would not be painting the interior of his townhome as well, he was enraged. Arguing loudly, he raged to the Board, "Why aren't you going to paint my townhome? After all, paint is paint!"

For that resident, *common* was conveniently defined by the service being performed—not by where it was appropriate or by who was paying. It did not occur to him that his assessments did not apply to anyone else's townhome interior being painted. In fact, he became even further enraged when one of the Board members asked him how he would feel if assessments were increased so that every home's interior could be painted. To him, that was ridiculous. He did not see that his request was just as inappropriate.

The opposite, yet comparable, misunderstanding was demonstrated by a homeowner in a multistoried condominium community.

**EXAMPLE:** The homeowner wanted to put a Jacuzzi on his balcony. He felt that since the balcony was part of his unit, he should be able to do whatever he wanted with it.

Just like the townhome owner in the paint example, the Jacuzzi-lover did not understand the meaning of common. In his case, he determined that common was anything not attached to his condominium unit. He simply chose to ignore the fact that because the balcony was outside, it was not his to do what he wanted.

Ultimately, after a great deal of explanation and argument, the Jacuzzi-lover understood—no Jacuzzi. The space on his balcony was clearly defined in the Association's documents as common. It was not his to change as he chose.

As you begin looking at what your Association does and is responsible for, ask the following questions.

- Do I have a full understanding of what is common to the Community?
- How well maintained are the common areas?
- What types of repair and maintenance schedules exist?
- What is the proper procedure (if there is one) for submitting repair or maintenance requests?
- How responsive is the Association when a repair or maintenance request is submitted?

Asking these questions will help you to understand this very important component of the Association's duties and responsibilities.

## Establish and Collect Assessments

Once you understand what constitutes the common areas and responsibilities of the Association, it is much easier to understand why there are assessments for the common expenses. Whether groundskeeping and landscaping, repair and maintenance of the common systems (such as plumbing, heating, and air conditioning), or the administrative expenses of keeping the business running, there are expenses for which everyone is responsible. These are the common expenses. The Association's expenses include the manager's fees, property taxes, gardeners, landscape designers, and every other vendor, consultant, or service purchased by and in support of the Community as a whole.

In every business, there are expenses (outflow) and revenues (income). The monetary income most commonly and regularly comes from the Association's assessments and the investment interest from your reserves. Other monies may come to the Association from previous litigation, commercial real estate revenues, or other sources.

Regular assessments are collected monthly. Only in cases when a problem of some kind arises or the need to avoid a future problem becomes apparent is there a need for special assessments.

Taking a look at the common expenses is one of the easiest ways to begin to understand the financial status of the Association. Be careful, though—if you are new to looking at an organization's expenses, everything will look like it costs too much. In some cases, that may be true, which means you can assist the Board, Committees, or manager to identify and reduce those expenses. In many cases, however, what seems exorbitant to you may actually be a usual and expected fee for the service provided.

**EXAMPLE:** One resident of a Community thought the fees for the financial services company that was overseeing the Community's reserves were too high. From his perspective, the Community was losing money by paying these "out of control" fees. In fact, when a comparative analysis was performed, it was found that the fees were well within the standard range. Later, everyone realized that the basis of the concern came from this resident's lack of business experience. He was accustomed to personal investment accounts and online investing only. He had no previous knowledge or experience with institutional fee structures.

As you look at the collection of assessments to pay for common expenses, you should ask yourself the following questions.

- How often do I pay my assessments?
- How are those assessments being used?
- How often and for what purpose have I needed to pay special assessments?
- What are the Community's regular, known expenses?
- Are those expenses justified or justifiable?

As you are asking these questions, you should also make sure that there is a budget for your Association, that the assessments cover the appropriate expenses, and that those expenses are within your budget. You should also determine if the Association can borrow against reserves. In many cases, such a loan is permissible as long as the monies are paid back within one year. It is best, of course, if the Association can avoid debt altogether.

Debt assumption and the availability of loans to Associations are relatively new fields of discussion. While monies are available, it is advisable that the Association not assume any debt. Of course, there will be situations in which debt is unavoidable. In those cases, however, the Association should examine its reserve amounts, its regular and known expenses, and its assessments. At that point, the Association should reassess its ongoing financial management and determine the steps that need to be taken to avoid such situations in the future.

## Ensure Adequate Reserves

As with the regular assessments, it is also the responsibility of the Association to make sure that there is enough money in reserve for the future needs of the property. Contrary to popular belief, these needs are not only predictable, but their replacement or upkeep should be scheduled, monitored, and managed.

Reserves are used for known and planned major capital expenditures. This may be a completely new security system, the redesign and decoration of the lobby area, a new roof for all buildings, or the repaving of the driveways. Whatever it is, it is a known and planned use of funds.

Reserve studies should be performed at least every three years— an interval that is usually defined in the Association's documents.

These studies usually take the form of a visual inspection of major components of the property, and they should be performed by an expert in the field. The study results should then be reviewed every year to make sure that if anything has changed—whether the change was because of the Association or was outside its control—the reserves will be adequate to cover upcoming expenses.

Do not make the mistake of thinking that the reserves are there for unexpected circumstances. Reserves are there for *planned* expenses. Special assessments are collected when something happens that catches the Community unaware. Unexpected circumstances lead to special assessments.

Although loans may be made to the Association from the reserve funds, they should be paid back within one year. While such borrowing may be unavoidable, it is best if the Association ensures that adequate reserve studies and reviews are performed in order to avoid such occurrences.

The reserve funds should be carefully invested. Because these are such important funds, the lower the risk, the better the investment. That does not mean you cannot earn money on your reserve funds. It just means that you should be careful about the level of risk you take in their investment.

Also, be careful about personal expertise when you are looking at investment advice for your reserves.

**EXAMPLE:** In one Community, a retired gentleman who had done well with his own investments in the market (and no longer had a lot to do) wanted to take over the investment strategy for his Community's reserves.

This was not a good choice. Just because he made money for himself did not mean that he understood how to invest the volume of monies that were held in reserves.

If you are going to seek investment advice, seek it outside of the Community. This lessens the potential for conflicts of interest. It also keeps the running of the Community clear. After all, it is usually the case that whoever manages the money manages the power, and can make more and greater decisions. By keeping the investment advice and management outside, there is far less risk of mismanagement of funds, or unhappiness and dissatisfaction within the Community.

As you look at the Association's responsibilities regarding reserves and future replacement of major components, ask the following questions.

- How much does the Association have in reserves?
- What is planned for the use of those reserves and when?
- Given what is planned, is there enough money?
- How are those reserves invested?
- Who is responsible for overseeing the investment of the reserves?

By asking these questions, you not only gain a greater understanding of the financial status of the Association, but you also begin to get involved in the future planning for the Community. You then become more active in the protection of your investment and your Community by understanding the investment strategy and oversight of the Association's reserves.

## Administer the Rules and Regulations of the Association

The fourth and final duty of the Association is to administer the rules and regulations of the Association. Of all the duties, this has the most pitfalls, causes the most anger and disagreement, and generally needs the most day-to-day attention.

No matter where you live, people are people. Someone will park where he or she should not, keep pets when the rules specifically do not allow them, and push the limits to see what he or she can get away with and for how long.

While that person may believe that what he or she is doing does not hurt or adversely affect anyone else, the fact is that rules and regulations exist for a reason. They are designed to protect all the residents and visitors of the property. They are designed to limit the liability and exposure of the Community, its residents, and its Association.

Whether those rules and regulations are in the form of the policies and procedures, the residents' handbooks, or the CC&Rs, the Association must ensure to the best of its ability that all of the rules and regulations are being followed. When they are not, action must be taken.

This is not to say that all rules and regulations are cast in concrete and cannot or should not be changed. Over time, some of the rules and regulations may not make sense any more. It may be that the time has come to look at those rules and regulations, and determine which of them make sense and which do not.

One of the brightest moments in the life of any Community and its Association is when its members are willing to make changes. Times change, people change, residents change, and the need for and applicability of certain rules and regulations may change as well. By making your Association a living, breathing entity that is always dedicated to and focused on the needs of the Community, you are doing yourself and your neighbors the greatest service possible.

One of the most common changes to the rules and regulations is regarding pet policies. When first built, many Communities made the decision not to allow pets in any of the units. The decision made sense, since pets can cause trouble both for the pet owner and for the neighbors. Everything from aggravating allergies and messing up the property, to the possibility of injury to residents or visitors, drove the Communities to make that decision.

Over time, however, people bring pets into their homes. They love them. They like to spend time with them. Those pets make the homeowners happy. Sometimes even the Board members have pets. So, what should the Association do? Should the Association not enforce its own rules and regulations?

Absolutely not. The one thing the Association must do is enforce the rules and regulations. They must be enforced regularly and equally. There must be consistency and fairness in the enforcement. There must be open communication with residents before, during, and after the enforcement process, to make sure that everyone understands what was done and why. There must also be open communication with the Community to ensure that there is no appearance of discriminatory behavior. Everyone must conform to the rules and regulations.

However, the Association should reevaluate whether the rules and regulations make sense. If so, keep them and enforce them consistently. If not, identify ways by which the rules or regulations should be changed to suit the changing needs of the Community.

As for the pets, maybe the rules stay the same and pets are still not allowed. If that is the case, without being punitive to those who pushed the envelope, possibly their pets are grandfathered in. In effect, their pets are allowed to stay until the end of their lives or until the resident moves. Once the pet has departed, it cannot be replaced.

Possibly, the demographics of the Community have changed and there is now justification and acceptance of pets. In that case, the pets already living in the Community are invited to stay and the door is opened to new pets for the other residents.

In any case, all the rules and regulations must be clearly delineated and communicated to all the residents of the Community— homeowners, renters, commercial property renters, and so on. Resident handbooks should be updated on a regular basis—possibly annually—to make sure that the rules and regulations described are still up to date.

Enforcement procedures and methods of enforcement should be described in detail. If there are any fees or disciplinary actions attached to particular violations, those should also be described.

Everyone should be playing on an equal playing field. It is the Association's responsibility to define and describe that playing field, and then to make sure that all the players know the rules. This is most easily accomplished through resident referendums on specific rules and regulations, legal opinions where necessary, and ongoing and consistent communication throughout the Community to make sure that everyone knows what is required and why.

As the Association goes forward in administering the rules and regulations, you should ask the following questions.

- ◆ What are the rules and regulations of the Association?
- ◆ How are the rules and regulations established and communicated?
- ◆ How often does the Association review the rules and regulations for necessary updates and changes?
- ◆ Are the rules and regulations of the Association enforced consistently?
- ◆ How can the Association improve the rules and regulations, and their enforcement, timeliness, and applicability to the Community?

By asking these questions, you will be able to determine how well the Association is doing in establishing, maintaining, and enforcing its guiding principles in the form of its rules and regulations. You will also find numerous opportunities for improvement in the Community. The more you find out about how your Community and Association can be improved, the better the living conditions for you and all of your neighbors and friends.

# —3—
# KNOWING THE PLAYERS OF THE ASSOCIATION

Now that you know how the Association is structured and the purposes it serves, it is necessary to understand the positions and players that, in effect, run and support the business. These are the Board of Directors, the Committees, and the management.

The most important thing to realize from the start is that all of these people are on your side. It may not always seem that way—after all, you may have wanted a different decision or recommendation than what was made. However, they are using their best judgment and intent to create and maintain a successful Community and Community Association.

If you find yourself regularly questioning their decisions or the outcomes of their decisions, then that is a cue for you to start becoming involved. Whether it is the condition of the property, frequent special assessments, or specific policies or procedures that are the catalyst for your questions, the more that you understand about what they do and how they do it, the more easily you can get involved or get your questions answered when they arise.

## THE BOARD OF DIRECTORS
The single most visible and responsible group is the Board of Directors. Generally, the Board is responsible for the strategy and management of the Community. It is responsible for making all the business decisions that affect the Association. It has fiduciary responsibility, legal oversight, and overall management responsibility for all of the Association's business.

The decision to become a member of the Board is not an easy decision to make. Board members choose to spend their own time working on behalf of the Community. They are interested not only in protecting their own investments, but also in protecting and enhancing the investments and living environments for all the residents of the Community.

The Board of Directors has decision-making authority for the Association. Depending upon the governing documents, that authority may be broadly defined or highly specific. In many cases and in many ways, the Board of Directors has comparable responsibilities to those of corporate officers.

In an Association, however, homeowners have a more immediate benefit not always available to their public sector counterparts. By being a member of the Association, homeowners have the opportunity and ability to immediately access and review the legal, financial, and management documents for the Community.

It is the responsibility of every homeowner to ensure that their investment is protected. One of the best and easiest ways to do so is to be actively involved in the Community—attending Board meetings, becoming a member of a Committee, asking questions of management, and more. That way, not only are you working to preserve, protect, and enhance your own property, but you are also protecting yourself and your neighbors from any unexpected and unacceptable surprises.

## Board Elections

The Board of Directors is elected into office. Depending upon how your Association's governing documents are written, elections may take place annually, every other year, every three years, and so on. Sometimes, when the elections are annual, they only affect some of the Board members. This creates a revolving membership with some members staying in office. It also gives some continuity to the process.

Depending upon how your Association is governed, the officers of the Board may only have a short time in office. This is something to which you should give attention. One of the problems of many

Boards is that people are moving in and out of office before the projects set in motion are completed. This can cause dissent when the new Board members come in.

Some Board members want the agenda to reflect their agenda. If that means the projects already in progress are in their way, they may work to stop or slow those projects. They do this thinking that their agenda is important and must be given close attention. Once again, their intentions are good, but their methods work against the Community.

The problem is that the Association needs continuity to operate successfully. Unless it is determined that previous Board members have been working in bad faith toward the Community and its Association, there must be completion to the projects voted upon by previous Boards and consistency to the way the Board and the Association operate.

If these type of problems arise, it may be necessary to change the Community's rules regarding how long members may serve or how frequently elections are held. As a member of the Community, you must ensure that the election system is designed to benefit the Community in every way.

## The Governing Documents

The role and responsibilities of the Board are defined in the governing documents of the Association. As you begin looking into the role of the Board and the decisions it is making, look first at the governing documents to fully understand the span of control afforded to the Board.

**EXAMPLE:** In one large Community, the Board of Directors was making decisions, going forward on behalf of the Community, and generally doing a good job. One day, however, a new homeowner attended a Board meeting and at every turn, kept saying, "Wait, you can't do that!" From her perspective, the Board was far outreaching itself and its authority in making decisions about everything from the budget to the upkeep of the property.

She thought that each resident had one vote and that the Board was just there to run the meetings and keep the files and documents of the

Association. To her, they were not an elected body specifically designed to oversee the business of the Community, but were instead there as an administrative support system to coordinate homeowner needs.

Upon being directed to review the applicable sections of the governing documents, she then understood the extent and span of responsibilities held by the Board. When asked where her initial understanding came from she explained that, previously, she had lived in a very small Community where each resident was on the Board and each person, therefore, had one vote. Her experience and the governing documents of her former Community taught her that the one-resident-one-vote system was the overriding system in all Community settings.

By guiding her through the governing documents and allowing her to learn and ask questions, Board members ensured that her concerns were addressed. Subsequently, by joining a Committee, she found a way to continue being active without being disruptive to the Board's operations.

## Responsibilities of the Board

The Board of Directors is responsible for establishing the policies for the management oversight of the Community, the Association, and the property in general. The Board may decide that some of those responsibilities will be delegated to a management company or manager. Even in that situation, the Board still holds ultimate responsibility for monitoring and overseeing those activities. In simplest yet broadest terms, the Board is the entity responsible for protecting, preserving, and enhancing the value of the property.

The Board is supported by the Committees. These Committees are responsible for bringing recommendations for action to the Board. The Board has the ultimate decision-making authority to determine which of those recommendations will be acted upon.

The responsibilities of the Board are many. They include, but are not limited to, the following:

- overseeing the finances of the Association, including establishing and managing an annual budget;
- ensuring that there is an annual audit by an outside Certified Public Accountant (CPA);
- establishing and collecting assessments from all homeowners;

- establishing reserves and ensuring that a professional reserve study is performed every three years, and its results reviewed each year;
- opening and maintaining association bank accounts with designated signatories;
- establishing, amending, communicating, and enforcing the rules and regulations of the Association;
- developing and overseeing comprehensive risk management procedures;
- ensuring the adequate upkeep and operation of the property;
- determining and obtaining appropriate insurance;
- paying for all authorized services to the Association;
- monitoring and overseeing all vendor activities, including undertaking an annual review of vendors for the Association;
- establishing and supporting Committees; and,
- designating, hiring, and firing personnel.

In looking at this list, it is easy to understand why Board members so often feel overwhelmed. Invariably, when people decide to join the Board, they usually do so because they feel that there is something they can offer that the Community needs. They often do not know how comprehensive the requirements are, and how much knowledge and understanding is required in order to fully perform their duties—or how satisfying it is to make that contribution to their Community.

## Officers of the Association

To a certain extent, the individual requirements are lessened as a result of the individual officer positions on the Board. These positions include the President, Vice President, Secretary, and Treasurer.

### President

The President of the Board is equivalent to the Chief Executive Officer (CEO) of a corporation. Ultimately, management and strategy responsibility lies within this position. Although the President (or any other Board member) cannot absolutely ensure success of the

Association or the Community, the greatest responsibility for the ongoing success of the Community and its Association rests with the President of the Board.

The President sets the tone for the Association and the Community. It is the President, as a role model, who makes it clear to all residents that the purpose of the Board is to preserve, protect, and enhance the Community and all of its residents. The duties of the President of the Board include, but are not limited to, the following:

- overseeing all Board and Committee activities;
- tracking and monitoring vendor activities;
- signing checks for expenses related to the Association;
- working with management to ensure adequate support for the Community;
- determining the agenda for each Board meeting;
- ensuring that the Board records are completed and distributed at least one week prior to the Board meeting;
- being available to residents to answer their questions and learn their concerns; and,
- writing newsletter articles giving updates on the activities of the Board and how the residents can be of assistance.

As you can see, the role of the President is as much one of public relations as it is of head of the business. The President is the most visible representative of the Community and to the Community. The importance of the role and its responsibilities cannot be overstated.

### Vice President
Second in command to the President is the Vice President of the Board. This person fulfills all the President's responsibilities when the President is absent. In addition, the Vice President is often responsible for directly overseeing and monitoring the work of the Committees. In such cases, the Vice President ensures that all Committee recommendation forms, reports, tracking documents, and the like are submitted to the Board in time for review at the next Board meeting.

## Secretary

The Secretary plays a pivotal role for the Board and the Community, because the Secretary is the keeper of the papers. All documents, minutes, and records of any kind are the responsibility of the Secretary. This is more than an administrative position. The Secretary—by ensuring that the minutes are taken correctly, records are in order and stored safely, and any records can be accessed at any time—acts as a legal protection for the Community and the Association. In the event of any legal action, the better the Secretary has set up and maintained the records, the easier it is for the Association to assist in its representation.

Minutes are *discoverable* documents. This means that in the case of litigation, Board and Committee meeting minutes can be requested by the other side's attorney—and they will be. By knowing in advance that meeting minutes can make the difference in a lawsuit, it becomes much more clear why the minutes need to be taken accurately and in an unbiased way.

Minutes are the means by which the Association tracks itself, as well as the means by which homeowners can keep regular track of what is—and is not—going on. They can also be part of your first line of defense in showing documentation that the Association has done what it said it would do.

The writing of meeting minutes is one of the ways by which personal agendas can most easily be identified. As the minutes for each Board meeting are being reviewed before being accepted, it is worthwhile for all involved to look for any discrepancies or apparent biases that might hurt the Association. Many Communities have been legally brought to their knees because of badly written or biased Board meeting minutes.

## Treasurer

The Treasurer is responsible for overseeing the Association's financial affairs. The duties and responsibilities of the Treasurer range from collecting assessments and dealing with delinquent assessments to assisting in the selection of an auditor. The Treasurer must provide a monthly report on the financial status of the Association. Any concerns should be brought to the Board's attention. In addition, expenses that may lead to special assessments or the use of reserves, whether planned or unplanned, should be presented by the Treasurer.

These are not the only members of the Board. While these members have specific responsibilities associated with their offices, they, along with all of their Board colleagues, should act as liaisons with the various Committees established and supported by the Board of Directors.

As you begin looking at your Board of Directors and how it operates, ask the following questions.

- ◆ How many members are there on the Board of Directors?
- ◆ How often are elections held?
- ◆ How many Board members are affected at each election?
- ◆ What is the impact of the election schedule for the Board and how does the schedule affect the smooth running of the Association and its projects?
- ◆ What are the responsibilities of the Board as described by the governing documents?
- ◆ How well does the Board fulfill those responsibilities as defined?
- ◆ Are there changes that should be made to the governing documents so that the Board can operate more efficiently and effectively in support of the Association?
- ◆ In which areas might the Board improve its performance as defined by the governing documents?
- ◆ Who are the officers of the Board?
- ◆ How are their positions defined?
- ◆ What specific roles or support do the officers provide to the Board and to the Community?

## COMMITTEE SUPPORT

For larger Communities, the primary support system for the Board of Directors is the Committees. Committee membership is made up of homeowners not serving on the Board of Directors. However, each Committee should have a dedicated Board member as a part of the Committee. The Board member attends the meetings, provides guidance, oversees the Committee's activities, and assists in executing and monitoring progress of those recommended actions that the Board has approved.

The Committees are an extension of the Board. They research the needs of the Community and make recommendations regarding how those needs can be met. Because there are a number of Committees and each consists of several people, the Committees also represent a cross-section of the Community. This gives the Community and all of its residents a greater and more representative voice to the Board.

The Committees should not make decisions or take actions of their own volition. They are designed to make recommendations only. Those recommendations must be complete and specific so that the Board can make informed decisions. However, it is the Board that makes the decisions.

This is a protection both to the Committee members and to the Association. As a business, the Association is protected from liability in certain cases. This protection extends to the Board members if they are insured under a Directors and Officers (D&O) or other insurance policy. By keeping the decision-making power at the Board level, the Committee members do not have to be concerned about their personal liability. They are providing information and recommendations only. The Board is the entity that makes the decision.

## Number and Types of Committees

One of the easiest ways to find unnecessary complexity in the operations of your Association is to look at the number and types of Committees that have been established. If there are more than five ongoing Committees, and if each of those Committees has more than five members, you have a complex structure.

There are two types of Committees: Standing Committees and Ad Hoc Committees. *Standing Committees* are authorized by the Board and operate on a continuous and ongoing basis. *Ad Hoc Committees* are established to look at a very specific issue or problem, and once they have done so, discontinue their efforts.

Depending upon the resources you consult, you will see that Associations can have as many as twelve Committees. This should be avoided, as it leads to too many simultaneous projects for the Association to deal with competently. Also, from a purely logistical standpoint, that many Committees is far too difficult and time-consuming for the Board to manage.

As a result, it is recommended that you have no more than five Standing Committees. These Committees are:

- Architectural;
- Legal;
- Financial;
- Communications; and,
- Social.


Standing Committees have greater and broader responsibilities to the Board than Ad Hoc Committees. They provide ongoing guidance and support, assisting the Board members in understanding the current and emerging needs of the Community, and in taking appropriate action.

Ad Hoc Committees, because they are established for a specific purpose, should have defined start and stop dates along with concrete goals. Because the Board will have to manage and oversee these Committees, you are well advised to keep the number of Ad Hoc Committees to a minimum at any one time. Also, if you find that there is an increasing need for Ad Hoc Committees, that is a cue to look at the Standing Committees' charters to see if they should be expanded to address the growing Ad Hoc activities.

Whether Standing or Ad Hoc, each Committee should have a specific, defined charter. These charters provide the Committee members with guidelines of the expectations for the Committee, as well as the parameters within which they must work.

Also, as noted, Board members should be prepared to serve either as members of Committees or as active liaisons between specific Committees and the Board. This way, the Committee is assured that it is getting Board attention. The liaison Board member is also able to provide immediate insight and guidance to the Committee to assist it in fulfilling its responsibilities.

## Architectural Committee

The Architectural Committee provides guidance to the Board regarding the architectural needs and standards for the Community. These include, but are not limited to, the preservation, safety, and enhancement of the physical and aesthetic environment, as well as the procedures for submission, review, and approval of architectural plans.

For example, the Association may set specific standards regarding colors and materials for the buildings in a Community. It may require certain landscaping or roofing, or specific types of window shades or drapes. These would be reviewed and discussed by the Committee before making their recommendation to the Board for adoption.

The Committee's tracking and monitoring of the enforcement of architectural standards and Board-approved projects that are underway is of great importance. The Committee works with the Board and management to develop and implement programs that promote the safety and security of the Community.

## Legal Committee

The Legal Committee evaluates and monitors legal actions related to the Community. It provides guidance to the Board through its review of rules and regulations related to Community, Association, and Board operations. This includes, but is not limited to, a review of rules and rule enforcement, amicable settlement procedures for possible rule violations, and updates and changes to the governing documents. It also includes the tracking and monitoring of consistent enforcement procedures.

This Committee is sometimes used as an informal method of reaching compromise between owners, or between owners and management, before disputes get out of hand. If a pet issue is a concern, the Legal Committee might review legislation regarding pets, such as local or state ordinances or the Fair Housing Act, or it might evaluate grandfathering risks and requirements before making a recommendation to the Board for decision.

This Committee is also responsible for the review of insurance policies and claims history. Recommendations from this Committee include the ways by which real and potential legal and financial risk can be reduced.

## Financial Committee

The Financial Committee provides guidance to the Board through its ongoing review of the financial status of the Community, as well as its recommendations regarding means of improving that financial position. This is accomplished through the Committee's proposed annual budgets and monitoring of Association finances. Monitoring activities include, but are not limited to, scheduling and overseeing outside audits, conducting reserve reviews and vendor reviews, and tracking project finance and proposed budget justification. This Committee also provides support, analysis, and information resources when projects requiring financial expenditure are proposed.

For example, a construction or remodeling project may require funding beyond what was expected or planned. In such cases, the Financial Committee would recommend the source of funding for the proposed project, such as the sale of assets (e.g., stocks and bonds), a special assessment, or a loan.

## Communications Committee

The Communications Committee is the primary liaison between the Board, the Committees, and the Community. This Committee is responsible for all the means by which the Community is kept apprised of Board- and Association-approved activities. Newsletters, notices, calls for input by the Board and Committees, and so on, are designed, implemented, managed, and monitored by the Communications Committee.

The newsletter published by this Committee plays a pivotal role in helping make the Community a true community. Included is information on rules changes; personal notes of births, marriages, or deaths; and, any other information that members want communicated to other members. The newsletter is also the most direct method for the Board and Committees to communicate progress and to gain greater participation from the homeowners.

In providing guidance to the Board, this Committee is responsible for recommending improvements to the ways by which information is disseminated to the Community and received by the Board and Committees. This includes follow-up mechanisms and Community response.

## Social Committee

The Social Committee is responsible for setting the tone and fostering the sense of community enjoyed by all of the residents of the Community. The Committee recommends, oversees, and reviews Community-sponsored activities, social programs, new member welcome events, and so on. Working together with the Communications Committee, the Social Committee ensures that all Community members are informed of upcoming events and activities well in advance. In providing guidance to the Board, this Committee is responsible for recommending means of expanding the sense of and participation by the Community.

As you look at your Committees, their structure, and responsibilities, ask yourself the following questions.

- How many Committees exist in the Association? Which are Standing Committees? Which are Ad Hoc?
- How many members serve on each Committee?
- What do the Committees do?
- Who is responsible for overseeing their activities?
- How do the Committees report on their findings and to whom?
- Do Committees in the Community make decisions on their own or do they bring their recommendations to the Board?
- How do the members of the Board interact with the Committees?
- How are members of the Community made aware of Committee membership opportunities? How often do new members join the Committees?

# MANAGERS AND MANAGEMENT COMPANIES

Probably the best documented and yet most controversial area of Association management is the area of the manager or management company. Most Communities either have or need a manager or management company to support their operations. That does not mean, however, that the decisions related to or the coordination with those entities run smoothly.

## Preventing Problems

One of the most consistent problems regarding the manager or management company and the Association is in understanding the relationship between the two. In many cases, the manager is not an employee of the Association. He or she may be an independent outside vendor or may belong to a larger management company. As a result, the Board members are not quite sure how to treat the manager—colleague, adversary, friend, or foe?

The answer is actually easy. You and your manager or management company are all on one side—the side of the Community and its Association. There should not be any adversity between the manager and the Community. After all, you are all trying to accomplish the same thing—the protection, preservation, and enhancement of the Community and its living environment.

Another common cause for adversity between the manager and the Association is when the Board members, knowingly or unknowingly, abdicate their responsibility to oversee the manager's activities. Just because a manager is brought in does not mean that the Board is no longer responsible for overseeing the needs of the Community.

In fact, the opposite is true. The Board and manager must work cooperatively to identify the needs of the Community, determine appropriate action, and then ensure that those actions are taken. The more the Board and manager work as a unit, the fewer the problems between the two.

When there is adversity, it usually stems from a misunderstanding of the role and responsibilities of the manager. The easiest way to address that misunderstanding is to go back to the beginning, and reevaluate and reestablish why you decided you wanted or needed a manager in the first place. From there, you can determine whether additional support is required, whether the person or company currently providing the support understands and fulfills your needs, and how best you, the Board, and your management support can work to ensure the safety and security of your Community.

## Outside Management

Running an Association—in fact, running any organization—is a highly time-consuming job. Every detail must be monitored and addressed. When there are problems, attention must be paid and action must be taken. If rules or regulations are broken, they must be enforced. These are the tasks and operations of the Association.

Depending upon your Community and its makeup, task management is often provided from within. Sometimes the President of the Board or another community member acts as a resident-manager for the Community. Even in these cases, the use and effectiveness of outside management support can be of great benefit to the Community and to the resident-manager.

The larger and more complex your Community, the more you need a support system for the management details. You really do not want to have to spend all of your time identifying, interviewing, and hiring vendors ranging from plumbers to gardeners. You may not have the connections and experience to be able to recommend everything from auditors to tracking and monitoring systems. You also probably do not want to be the person who has to confront or be confronted by your neighbor about an emotional issue.

Managers and management companies take care of all of these details and more. They are an external function performing an internal support role. As managers, they have a different, more operational perspective of the Community. They probably don't live in the Community they manage—which gives them the benefit of objectivity. They are employees, not neighbors.

They must be allowed to perform their duties with the guidance, understanding, and support of the Board and the Community. This does not mean that the Board abdicates its responsibilities to the manager. The manager is an operational arm for the Community. The Board remains responsible for the strategy, health, and overall management and oversight of all things related to the Association and the Community.

## Manager Responsibilities

There are four major categories of manager responsibility: property maintenance, service, administration, and finance. As you can see, these categories cover all the major areas of responsibility for the property and the Association.

It is important to note that these responsibilities are performed by the manager—whether a resident, part of a management company, an individual employee, or an outside vendor. It is up to the Board—with the assistance of the Committees—to determine the needs of the Community and Association regarding those areas for which some form of support is required.

Realistically, there is no way to create a comprehensive list of managerial duties—particularly because the specific tasks performed within those duties vary within each Community. However, the following is an overview of some of the components generally included in each of the four categories cited.

### Property Maintenance

The manager is responsible for inspecting common property areas, as well as any components of individual properties that are the responsibility of the Association. The manager is also responsible for ensuring that the Association is in compliance with all laws and ordinances associated with the property, as well as taking or recommending actions to be taken to ensure that requirements are met.

### Service

The manager is responsible for ensuring that there is regular and adequate trash and garbage collection, landscape maintenance, and pest control. If your Community has any security services, it is the responsibility of the manager to identify and oversee their activities. Water and other utility services are also overseen by the manager, including negotiating with local providers for reduced costs whenever possible.

## *Administration*

Administration is an ongoing and often tedious task of the Association. Some of the manager's most basic tasks include emergency call service, as well as complaint processing and resolution. In working with existing or proposed vendors, the manager establishes or complies with contracting procedures for bid invitations and their analysis, followed by the negotiations with, and monitoring and inspection of, the vendors' work. Vendor payment is also handled by the manager.

As part of the administrative activities in support of the Board and its volunteers, the manager prepares the annual report and other legal documents, ensures that meeting minutes are completed and signed in a timely manner, follows up on Board orders and requests, and generally provides any additional support the volunteer leadership requires.

## *Finance*

The manager is responsible for preparing operating budgets and other financial documents for the Board's review, collecting assessments and user fees, and disbursing monies in accordance with the Board-approved budget. The manager ensures that the checking and other Association accounts are maintained and reconciled, and prepares periodic financial statements for Board review, including income and expense comparisons. The manager is also responsible for providing assistance to the Association's accountant and the independent auditor.

As you can see, many of these functions ally closely with those of the Board and Committees. When a manager is at his or her best, it is most apparent in the almost invisible execution of the Board's decisions and the consistent support leading to those decisions.

## Choosing Manager Support

While the arena of managers and management companies is well documented, there has not been a great deal written about exactly when to look for management support or what you are looking for once you begin the search. As a result, this has left most Communities scrambling to find adequate support once a problem—usually a big one—occurs.

In order to avoid this scenario, the following is a logic system for choosing the type and source of management support for your Community. It will help you determine when you should start looking for outside support and the changes in support you may need as you go. As you start this process, look at the needs, history, and complexity of your Community, and make an educated decision about the support and services you require. From there, choose from the three most common management options: self-management, independent management, and management company.

## Self-Management

You may choose a do-it-yourself or self-management structure. This is only appropriate for very small Associations. While it may seem like the simplest option, it often has hidden pitfalls. Self-management relies upon the skills and generosity of the Association members. This is not a problem if they have the time and talent to handle the business needs of the Association, which can be urgent and time-consuming.

Self-management also crosses into areas of self-interest. Can your management team remain neutral on complex issues or will their opinions and vested interests potentially have a negative impact on the Association?

Will Association members be paid for their services? If they are not paid, will they have sufficient motivation to get the job done in a timely manner? (Remember, the Association's credit and reputation depend upon the manager's business acumen.)

How will matters be handled when the manager takes a vacation or moves? If your manager fails to perform, how will he or she be dismissed from the position without creating disruption and resentment within the Association?

These and other issues must be carefully considered before choosing the self-management option.

## Independent Manager

If your Association has a dynamic and involved Board of Directors, an independent manager might provide an effective level of management to meet your needs.

To find an independent manager, the Board conducts a search, having established how much experience the prospective manager needs and what that experience is worth to the Association in salary, benefits, and other compensation.

Once a suitable candidate has been found, the Board negotiates and reviews the manager's fees and retains responsibility for most business decisions, including establishing the limits to the manager's authority. In some cases, the manager charges a monthly flat fee for services provided as an independent contractor. In others, the manager becomes an employee of the Association.

Typically, an independent manager provides some direct services, such as financial accounting, recordkeeping, and reporting, and also oversees and monitors outside vendors for legal, maintenance, and other matters.

The manager answers to the Board, and the Board must review the manager's annual contract. The Board must also make provisions for the manager's absence due to vacation or illness.

## Management Company

For large Associations or those with minimal Board participation, a management company can be hired to take over the entire management responsibility for the Community. The company reports to the Board of Directors.

In such cases, the management company provides a project manager who may be on- or off-site. The company hires other employees, contracts with vendors, and directs all maintenance, improvements, and services.

This relieves the Board members of much of the burden of day-to-day management, though the management company does not usurp the role of the Board. The Board continues to be responsible for the legal, financial, and operational success of the Community and its Association.

The Board will decide to bring in a management company so their responsibility can remain at the oversight level without having to be involved in or concerned with the daily details of the Association.

Ultimately, the core issue for the Board in making the decision between an independent manager or a management company becomes the Board members' comfort with handing over responsibility to a company to such an extent that they have less voice in the ongoing operations of their Association.

On the other hand, one of the benefits of a management company is that it maintains consistent levels of service through the inevitable cycles of Board, owner, and employee turnover. This consistency can make it easier for the Association to operate in the long run.

## The Necessity of Management

No matter what the size of your Community, some form of management is required. With that understanding, it becomes easy to make objective assessments about the needs of the Community, the resources currently available, and the actions that need to be taken to fulfill those needs. The good news is there are so many support systems available that no matter what your needs, you will be able to find a management company or manager to fulfill them.

As you look at your Association and how it is currently managed, ask the following questions.

- ◆ How is your Association currently managed?
- ◆ Which of the management duties are performed internally by a resident manager?
- ◆ Which of the duties are performed by outside resources?
- ◆ What types of problems have there been either in the management of the Association or in the relationship between the manager and the Board?
- ◆ How might those problems be better addressed?
- ◆ How does your Community fit into the logic structure?
- ◆ Do the services you currently receive from outside resources match those recommended? (Should they?)
- ◆ What improvements to the management of the Association do you recommend?

# −4−
# THE LEGAL STRUCTURE
# OF THE ASSOCIATION

Legal issues pervade all aspects and activities of a Community Association. Clearly, the creation of the Association itself and its Declaration or CC&Rs, Articles, Bylaws, and Rules necessitate professional legal counsel. The hiring of employees and dealing with labor unions can require special legal skills in employment law. Construction permits and zoning variances sometimes can be resolved with someone other than a lawyer, but the expense incurred for legal counsel is generally worth it.

Expensive and needless litigation can be avoided by the sensible use of legal counsel, which will also minimize the exposure of the Association and its Board to liabilities. Consequently, the need for competent legal counsel is ongoing.

The relationship between the Board of Directors, management, and the Association's legal counsel is crucial to the legal safety of the Association and the individual homeowners. Only by taking the time to fully determine the community's legal needs and identify the best resources can the Association fully preserve, protect, and enhance itself.

## LEGAL COUNSEL
Legal counsel is not a luxury for a Community Association—it is a necessity. Such counsel should preferably be a law firm rather than a sole or duo law practice. A firm provides broader support in differing expertise and backup personnel.

It is essential that legal counsel be truly objective and have no conflicts of interest. Therefore, no owner or family member of an owner should be legal counsel under any circumstances, even with a written waiver of any conflict. Because of the very personal nature of Associations, it is wise not to risk emotional clashes by having any owner or family member as a vendor and especially as legal counsel. Any savings in money by using family or friends can be offset by horrendous problems down the line.

While legal counsel should always be independent, objective, and free of conflicts of interest, the size of the Community sometimes determines the relationship between the Association and its counsel. When small Associations are managed by professional management companies, the Board should determine if the management company has legal counsel on retainer or an ongoing relationship. The Board should find out who that counsel is, and whether or not there is any conflict with any of the owners or the Association. Mid- and large-sized Associations should have general counsel upon whom they call for their legal needs.

The standing Legal Committee of the Association should have a Board member serving as liaison. This Committee actively reviews and makes recommendations regarding legal issues facing the Association. In this way, the Board does not waste its time acting as a legal specialist, and it simply receives suggestions from the Legal Committee.

There are generally two types of legal counsel serving Associations—those who specialize in or understand Community Association law, and those in the area of corporate law. Most Associations are subject to the corporate laws of the state where they are located. Therefore, it is beneficial to the Association to engage a law firm that has the ability to serve the Association's needs both in the area of Community Association law and in general corporate law.

## THE ASSOCIATION'S LEGAL NEEDS

The general legal needs of an Association fall into two general types: the external legal issues and the internal legal issues.

External legal issues are those involving contracts between the Association and its vendors. The Association's dealings with government agencies, such as workers' compensation, departments of building and safety, zoning commissions, health departments, and other regulatory bodies, fall into this category.

Lawsuits brought by or against the Association raise external legal issues, as well. When the Association is sued, the first determination to be made is whether or not the claim is covered by insurance, and whether or not the insurer should provide defense counsel. When the Association wants to file a lawsuit, it must determine if an hourly or contingent fee should be the compensation for the attorney.

Lawyers are paid contingency fees when they accept a percentage of the recovery, if there is any. If there is no recovery, there is no fee. Contingency fees can account for the lawyer's full fee, or may be paid in conjunction with an hourly fee. By accepting a contingency fee, the lawyer is sharing the risk with the client.

Internal legal issues can be divided in two fundamental areas as well. First, the governing documents—CC&Rs, Bylaws, and House Rules (guidelines for conduct in common areas and relationships between unit owners)—must be established and may be modified from time to time. The manner in which they are applied to the owners and the Association itself can create thorny questions.

Second, the enforcement of these governing documents requires a great deal of care. The Association must ensure that there is consistency in the way that the governing documents are enforced. There can be no appearance of impropriety or special treatment. Due process—which is explained more fully on page 58—must also be applied to protect the Association.

Deciding to use an alternative to litigation through the courts is an increasingly favored means of resolving any external or internal issues involving an Association. Mediation or arbitration can be chosen to bring about a fast, fair, and final result.

While both of these methods are described in Chapter 5, the easiest way to differentiate the two is that *mediation* is the use of a neutral third party to help solve the dispute through discussion and negotiation, while *arbitration* is like a trial but in less formal proceedings. There are benefits and risks to any dispute resolution procedure, so it is always in the Association's best interests to discuss the options with its lawyer before proceeding.

# THE IMPORTANCE OF LEGAL COUNSEL

Whether your Association needs legal advice on routine contract matters or on pending litigation, your lawyer may be influencing decisions worth many thousands of dollars. Beyond monetary costs, legal issues may affect the long-term well-being of your Association. Therefore, it is important that you make an informed, careful decision, and select legal counsel you can trust. Consider these suggestions as you proceed.

- Unless they are involved in a specific legal matter facing the Association, a member of the Board of Directors and the Association manager (if any) will most likely be designated to interview and select counsel. A minimum of three people should participate in the interviews and decision-making for the recommendation to the Board.

- Referrals should be sought from other Community Associations, other lawyers, or local bar association referral agencies. Lawyers who have a vested interest in the Association, such as owners, residents, or lenders, may be consulted for referrals, but not considered as candidates for Association counsel, due to potential conflicts of interest.

- Community Association law is highly specialized. It is important to select a lawyer who is experienced in handling the general legal issues affecting Community Associations, but who is also willing to refer the Association to another professional if a legal matter needs special knowledge.

Following is a selection of questions you could pose to potential candidates. It is not meant to be complete, but rather to give you some interviewing guidelines.

- What experience do you and your firm have representing Community Associations?

- What experience do you and your firm have handling the specific legal matter confronting our Association?

- As a Community Association lawyer, what types of services would you provide?

- Do you have other affiliations—such as with other Associations, management companies, vendors, developers, professional associations—within the Community Association industry?
- How is your firm organized in terms of delegation of responsibility for our Association's legal work?
- Does your firm have a policy regarding returning telephone calls? What is it?
- If necessary, are you prepared and qualified to represent our Association in a court of law?
- Have you or your firm had any malpractice claims made against you? Are you covered by malpractice insurance?
- What is your billing policy, including rates for you and others in your firm, billable time increments, retainers, billing frequency, and itemization of costs?
- What are some ways for our Association to reduce our legal costs?
- Can you provide us with references from current and former Association clients?
- Why should our Association hire you as our legal counsel?
- Are there any questions you would like to ask us?

Interview all of the candidates and talk about your impressions before you make a decision. Remember that the temperament of the attorney is important as well. Observe the conduct of the attorney, keeping in mind that people put their best foot forward in an interview. Intemperate and hostile counsel can cause problems and prolong issues by offending owners, renters, vendors, and staff.

Once a lawyer has been chosen, one person from the Association should be designated to communicate with the counsel on all matters. That person should be prepared to take notes and report back to the Board, as well as to participate in the review of your counsel's billings.

Legal questions can arise without warning. It is better and less costly to do your homework now and conduct your interviews before you need a lawyer. To rush through the process and make a hasty decision when you are confronted with problems can be disastrous.

Legal questions arise at every Board meeting. However, not all of them require legal counsel. These questions should be discussed by the Board, and if there is any doubt about whether or not legal counsel should be utilized, the Board should give the benefit of the doubt to having legal counsel address the issue.

Some Boards want legal counsel to sit through all of the meetings. This can be a waste of Association funds if the attorney is only needed to discuss a specific topic or issue. However, it may be necessary for an attorney to sit through complete meetings if there are difficult members or others who are intent on causing trouble.

## AVOIDING LEGAL PROBLEMS WITHIN THE ASSOCIATION

While there is no way to completely avoid having legal difficulties, when the Board of Directors and Association management work together cooperatively, some of those problems can be headed off before they escalate.

### Board of Directors

Board members must constantly remind themselves of their independent, fiduciary duties to the Association and its members, in order to avoid personal liability. *Fiduciary duty* is the highest personal duty of one person toward the financial affairs of another. Beyond this high level of trust and responsibility, the Board must take action on issues that arise—whether legal or otherwise. The Board must act immediately to remedy claimed violations or the courts may find that they have waited too long. The court will apply the rules and procedure it would apply to any business entity under the principles of corporate law.

One of the functions of that body of law is the protection of the interests of shareholders. This is emphasized when the shareholders are homeowners and the corporation is dealing with a very important part of a person's identity—one's home.

### Elections, Voting, and Board Responsibility

The number of votes it will take to pass a motion for the Board to do something will become evident quite quickly. The negotiation among Board members is part of the give and take that occurs in a democracy.

It is to be expected, and you should relish the idea that you can be a part of it by being a Board member, contacting a Board member individually, or speaking out in open meetings of the Association. At all times, acting reasonably is more likely to get positive results.

Because of the intensely personal nature of Associations, cliques form that, by proxy voting or campaigning, endeavor to keep themselves in positions of control. This can be a good thing if the clique or majority group is fair, runs the Association like a business, and is not malevolent. If the contrary is the case, then you must see to it that the other owners are informed of whatever the problem happens to be, and a campaign is started to correct the problem.

If the problems are really serious, then the options are to campaign for favorable Board members at the next annual election, or as a final measure, campaign for a recall election of some or all of the Board members.

Apathy of owners is quite often the most frustrating thing you may face in having owners vote in an election (annual or otherwise), run for the Board, serve on a Committee, or be involved at all. Consequently, the same few people may run things just because of others' lack of interest.

If you find that everything you have tried to correct a bad situation is to no avail, the court is the place for the final resolution of the matter. You can expect fairness—not perfection—but it may be expensive, as you will need legal counsel. However, it may be well worth it if the value of your property is at issue or if the quality of life in your home is in jeopardy.

## Law and the Goodwill of the Community

Going to court is expensive. Mediation is the best way to resolve such difficult problems, if both sides agree to this method of dispute resolution.

People of goodwill can disagree. This becomes apparent very quickly on the Board of a Community Association—and it can be a force to better the Community as a whole. Differing perspectives exchanged with the intent to help is one of the best, most collaborative ways to improve the Association and the Community.

People instinctively identify closely with their homes. Regardless of the emotional relationships with people who live there, and regardless of their home's physical condition, it is theirs. Even if they share hallways, parking areas, or recreation or laundry facilities, they feel strongly about the space that they call home. When they close the door on the world and say, in effect, *Home at last*, their identification with it is vital and understandable.

Channeling that strong identification of the owners for the good of all calls upon the skills of Board members and management. This is especially true of the latter, because they see more of the day-to-day activities of the owners than the Board does. Thus, good rapport between management and the Board is the necessary ingredient in establishing the same among the owners.

## MANAGEMENT

Every association should at all times have a competent manager or management company. Even temporary management by the Board or any of its members can be utterly disastrous because of the temptations of special treatment of Board members and special advantages given to them. The one thing you want to get away from is special treatment, because it breeds nothing but disaster—first psychological, then legal.

Good managers are vital to the success of an association. Consequently, Associations should avoid untrained or hostile managers or management companies. The Board must know that it is the ultimate authority for the Association and resist the temptation to become management's rubber stamp. It is common for managers to fill power vacuums created by passive Boards—this should be avoided at all costs.

### Management and the Community

Managers play a central role in the tone of the Community and its Association. The more professional and personable, the better, because the risks for the Association can be high when that relationship is tainted.

It is essential for management to avoid becoming embroiled in political disputes between groups of homeowners. Similarly, one of the most difficult things for the Board to avoid is management stacking the Board with puppets who do management's bidding. In that situation, the management—not the owners—is in control, and the temptations of corruption are real. This is where serious legal problems can arise.

Management must keep the owners informed of annual budgets, insurance, expenses, reserves, and investments, as well as changes in statutes and regulations affecting Community Associations. It may also be in charge of sending out delinquency notices or other reports of Association rule violation. At times, its letters may be offensive and its contact with owners disrespectful and hostile. If a disrespectful or hostile letter comes to an owner, there is every reason for the owner to complain and ask the Board to require better treatment. Whether an Association has a manager on the premises, an off-site manager, or a management company, the process is the same. It is simple, but hard. The Board sets policy within the boundaries of the governing documents—CC&Rs, Bylaws, statutes, and House Rules—and then must hold management accountable when something improper has been done.

## The Manager-Board Relationship

Boards rely heavily upon management to advise them on what to do under many circumstances, but this does not change the Board's duty to make decisions. The Board must absolutely require management to be accountable in the execution of Board policies and the treatment of individual owners.

Some managers may avoid accountability by simply failing to put the follow-through issues on the Board's meeting agenda. People then forget the issues, and if the Board allows managers to get away with doing that, the Association will eventually find itself in deep trouble.

Boards may change each year and there may be an institutional memory only with the manager. Such a situation can create serious problems if the finances are allowed to fall into disarray, if the mandated reserves are not accounted for, and if the delinquencies are not kept to a minimum.

Good managers will have no problem if a Board requires a management audit. Such an audit motivates management to be accountable, and can form the basis for giving a raise or a bonus. Sometimes it is the basis for revitalizing or even replacing management. Depending on its cost, such an audit should be undertaken about every three years, unless there are warning signs that it should be done sooner. Such audits are to be done for certain vendors as well, for the Association to be well run. Naturally, the accounting for the Association should be audited annually by a certified public accountant (CPA) who is not connected with the Association in any way.

Audits can be done for insurance, utilities, gardening, or any function of the Association's vendors, to stimulate accountability and minimize the temptation for corruption. Competitive bidding for vendors' contracts may reduce the need for audits. The key factor to remember is that the longer a manager or vendor has served the Association, the more there is a need for an audit.

Good managers are hard to find, and an Association should take good care of them and treat them well. On the other hand, if the manager is lazy or not trained, the Board should not hesitate to require a replacement as soon as possible. A manager or management company can make or break an Association.

Boards must treat management well. If there is good reason, a year-end bonus is certainly in order. If management does something extraordinary during the year that is not just a regular duty of management, some reward is a good business move. Boards and management should keep in mind that the Association is really a business and should be run that way. Boards can achieve much more by treating management professionally and with kindness.

In selecting a manager, Boards can handle initial interviews through a selection Committee or even an agency, but the Board itself should make its selection by interviewing the three or four top candidates. Boards should look for the experience and professional training of the candidates, but equally as important are the personality and the people skills that they possess.

Managers should be funded for a reasonable number of professional conferences and membership in appropriate management organizations. These benefits come back to the Association as dividends.

### The Manager/Homeowner Relationship

Managers must be even-handed in dealing with owners or their tenants. If a manager is giving some owners special treatment, that manager is creating present and future conflicts of interest. The manager will naturally expect something in return—such as a large year-end bonus or special time off—if a Board member is given special treatment such as parking preference, grace periods for Association payments, or other similar things.

As in any well-run business, an Association should require management to be accountable to the Board. A management audit, done by experts, will help the Board in understanding what it should be getting from management and also motivate management to be more responsive to the Board's requirements.

## PREVENTING LEGAL PROBLEMS

There is a tendency to view anything legal as if it is negative or in some way could not have been avoided. In Community Associations, the governing documents, in fact, provide a means of preventing legal problems from occurring—as long as they are enforced consistently and due process is applied.

Many legal problems can be avoided by taking steps such as acquiring proper insurance coverage for things such as workers' compensation, property, general liability, and Directors and Officers liability. In addition, the Association must ensure that there are no conflicts of interest between Board members, management, homeowners, vendors, and others that could lead to legal difficulties later.

The governing documents provide the skeleton or structure of the legal entity, but because the entity is dealing with human beings, it cannot function without the interaction of people. If members of the Association are given opportunities to give their views on how things should happen, there is less friction and many problems are avoided.

Members who are given a feeling of well-being in the Community Association setting are less likely to create conflicts and problems for the Association and its members. When people are given the opportunity to participate, there is a greater likelihood that problems will not occur—making homeowner participation one of the best preventive mechanisms to avoiding legal problems.

## COVENANTS, CONDITIONS, AND RESTRICTIONS (CC&Rs)

Covenants, Conditions, and Restrictions, usually referred to as CC&Rs, are the legal heart of any Community Association. They are the most important of the governing documents of an Association.

The CC&Rs are usually recorded with the local county recorder's office, and constitute the legal foundation of the nature of the Association, its purpose, its legal structure, and the limitations imposed on the kinds of activities of the Association. Most importantly, they determine under which statutes the Association will operate. This gives each owner a clear indication of the nature of the Association, as well as the things that are or are not allowed.

The CC&Rs are so basic to the operation of an Association that a majority of the total voting power of the owners must vote for a change in them. This tough standard is necessary to keep such a fundamental part of the Association from being tossed about on the whim of one Board or another.

When someone commits to buying into a Community Association, there are long-term expectations, which are based upon the CC&Rs. Those expectations should be fulfilled.

For example, if an Association has a restriction against pets except for birds and fish, and someone wants to have a cat, this should not be allowed. If that person wants to keep a cat, he or she must go to where cats are allowed. Owners must keep in mind that the many benefits of Association living require compromises.

The CC&Rs establish the owners' property rights, including definitions of the common areas, how the use of the owners' property may be restricted, and the owners' obligations to the Association. They provide for rules enforcement, the

Association's powers, all financial matters, and reserve funds, among other important aspects of the life of the Association.

It is imperative that every potential owner examine all of the governing documents before buying into an Association—especially the CC&Rs, and particularly those provisions covering pets, architecture, leasing, and other topics that may be of special interest to a buyer.

For example, if you are buying for investment purposes, you should examine any restrictions that may limit the value or marketability of your investment. This may include restrictions on leasing and subleasing, or restrictions on the number of people permitted to live within the various units.

Recreational facilities are often important to the value of property, and restrictions of their use may be a positive or negative factor for some people. For example, clubhouses are often used by the developer to sell properties, but afterwards they can be neglected and fall into disrepair. This is a very negative influence on future sales or leasing—not to mention the psychological effect on all of the residents.

For prospective owners, a quick examination of the CC&R table of contents will give you an overview of their scope and point out the areas that you may want to examine before you buy. Keep in mind that the CC&Rs have the most powerful control over how you live in a Community Association. If you have trouble with any part of them, you may want to choose to live in another Community more to your liking, since it is very difficult to make any changes to the CC&Rs.

While it is difficult, CC&Rs of existing Associations *can* be changed. Frequently, more than a simple majority is necessary to change the CC&Rs. If repeated attempts to change them end in failure, the only recourse is to petition a court for an order amending the CC&Rs. This process is very divisive and quite expensive. Sound leadership of the Board and its officers can help prevent these problems.

## BYLAWS

The Bylaws, another of the governing documents of an Association, are primarily concerned with the rights of Association members, their meetings, and details about the directors and officers. These logistical concerns are important, and a prospective member of the

Association should examine them carefully. Members of the Association should pay special attention to the qualifications for Board membership and the rights of members to inspect records—especially prospective members' rights to inspect the governing documents and current financial statement.

The Bylaws are as important as CC&Rs and sometimes as difficult to amend. They may not be recorded in the same manner as CC&Rs, because they do not necessarily deal with property rights. The management of the Association and the relationships between the owners are significant parts of the Bylaws, and should be examined before buying into an Association.

They have an impact on how your property may be used and enjoyed, and how other owners may affect it. They differ from the CC&Rs in that they usually contain no restrictions on the use of your property, but they may have important restrictions on your behaviors, such as noise and activity limitations.

## ARTICLES OF INCORPORATION

The *Articles of Incorporation* constitute another important set of governing documents that define the nature of the Association, its scope of powers, and its legal status. The Articles are usually filed with the secretary of state, and fulfill the legal requirements that the officers and directors are identified, and that the broad purposes or the nature of the corporation are set out. For example, the property tax assessment may depend upon the nature of the Association. Are all or part of the common areas owned as tenants in common? Are they owned by the Association? Who, then, is responsible for maintenance and replacement of facilities?

There is rarely a problem with the Articles of Incorporation that would concern an owner. Nevertheless, a careful buyer will examine them just to be on the safe side, and a copy may be required during purchase or refinance transactions.

Nearly all Community Associations are corporations, and are therefore subject to corporation laws, including their Articles of Incorporation. As a consequence, the restrictions on the delegation of duties and responsibilities of corporate directors are strictly enforced.

Those duties are generally the same as those for other corporate directors—unless the governing corporation law gives some immunities to nonprofit corporations and the Community Association involved qualifies. These considerations are the reasons why counsel experienced in corporation law should be engaged by the Association.

# HOUSE RULES

The provisions of CC&Rs and Bylaws are generally established with limited input from owners, but House Rules allow much more participation and flexibility. House Rules deal with the day-to-day upkeep and management of the common areas, including the recreational or parking areas. They are established by the Board as part of the governing documents, and may be amended or changed by it as changing conditions require.

It must be emphasized that the enforcement of these and all of the other rules is the duty of the Board. A breach of any rule should be taken seriously, whether or not it is a violation of any of the governing documents.

A troublesome owner is one who violates these rules simply because he or she does not think the rules apply to him or her. It is tempting to express one's individuality in a Community Association setting. One can do so—but generally inside the individual's property only.

A home is one's castle, but only in a limited way. The constitutional protections against unlawful search and seizure are maintained wherever a person is residing, even in a Community Association. The right to quiet enjoyment of one's abode is also preserved. The right of the Association to enter for emergency reasons and restrictions on exteriors of the property are two of the things that Community Associations have that other styles of living do not.

If you look at the recorded material related to a property, such as a single family residence, you will find many restrictions on the property. Easements for telephone lines, gas lines, utility lines, and rights of way for streets and roads are just a few examples of use restrictions on property. Another example of such impositions are assessments for lighting, schools, sidewalks, and public utilities. All of these are shared, in part, by all of the owners of a Community Association.

The provisions of House Rules are all for the mutual enjoyment of the owners and can be readily modified to meet changing circumstances. Such rules reflect the unique nature of each Association. Rarely are any two Associations identical. The geographical location—such as a seaside, mountain, or ski area—is a factor in the character of the Association. The nature of the Association—such as a retirement community or one devoted to horse or boat ownerships—is another factor influencing the rules. Any recreational facility, whether in a high-rise building or luxury townhouse setting, requires rules tailored for its specific needs.

Establishing or amending House Rules should be one of the best opportunities for the Association to practice the democratic process. Open meetings devoted solely to making or amending the rules are the best examples of this. Setting up a special Committee for that purpose is another way for the Board to involve many members who do not wish to devote the time to Board membership, but who want to be heard and can contribute to the Association and feel that they have a part in their own destiny in the Community. (Such meetings would require the usual notice provisions of the other governing documents, as well as the due process, or fundamental fairness, necessary for an open and democratic community.)

## INSURANCE

Protecting yourself from the risk of loss is one of the most crucial decisions your Association will have to make. It is very important that you get the best advice from an expert—your professional insurance agent or broker. An insurance *agent* customarily has an agreement with an insurance carrier, writes policies through that company, and can provide cost-effective package deals. An insurance *broker* shops around with numerous insurance carriers, gets the best coverage for the best price, and can obtain hard-to-get special coverages. There are advantages to using both of them, and the Board has to decide which to use.

Community Association living presents two interests that need protection—your own unit and the common areas. For example, in typical condominium ownership, the Association will have a master policy insuring the common areas. The premiums for such insurance are paid by the Association from owners' fees collected by the Association. Each owner is individually responsible for the insurance and premiums on each individual unit.

Governing documents, such as statutes, CC&Rs, and Bylaws, will dictate the interests for which you are responsible. Each Community Association is unique. Learn what is expected of you and the Association for your best protection.

Insurance coverage is available in two basic, general types. The first is property and the second is liability.

*Property insurance* gives protection from damage to or loss of personal and real property by fire, theft, and various other causes. The policies can be *all risk* or *named peril* policies. Where *all risk* insures for loss with specific exclusions, *named peril* insures only for specifically named causes of loss.

Ask your insurance broker or agent if your Association's policy or your personal policy contains a coinsurance clause. This clause may reduce the amount of recovery if the loss is not a total one. In certain circumstances, the owner or Association becomes a coinsurer for a loss. This kind of clause in a policy represents a contractual process that inhibits an insured from intentionally causing a loss. If your policy has such a clause, have your agent or broker explain it to you until you *really* understand the concept and how it can apply to you.

Naturally, the Association is concerned about insuring the real property of the Community. The unit owner is more concerned with real and personal property loss. Nevertheless, the insurance payments may vary in certain Communities, and you should verify these things as soon as you are able. There is usually a deductible for each loss, and the amount will affect the premium. You must decide what balance you need between these two factors—premiums and deductibles—in your policy of insurance.

*Liability insurance* protects the Association from claims for personal injury and property damage arising from activities and conditions involving the common areas. Such claims involving your own unit must be provided for by your own insurance policy.

Some Associations have a structure known as a *tenant-in-common ownership*. In such cases, each homeowner owns a percentage of the common areas, as well as his or her own unit. If you are a tenant-in-common owner of the common areas, you should be a named insured or an additional insured in the policy provided by the Association to cover the common areas. There should be little or no additional cost for this protection, because the facts surrounding a claim do not change merely because the real owners are given protection.

When you or the Association are sued, the greatest expense may be the cost of legal counsel. Such counsel is provided by the insurance company, and it takes complete control of such claims and suits. Board members must be especially vigilant in making sure that adequate insurance coverage is provided. That duty must not be delegated to management only. The Board must require accountability from management and its insurance experts to obtain the best protection for the best price—and see that they do it. This is true for all insurance coverages to protect the Association.

In the event of a loss affecting common areas as well as owners' areas, there are likely to be insurance adjusters from all of the insurances involved in what could be conflicting claims. Take care to identify your specific claims and issues, and work with the adjuster from your insurer. The insurer for the Association may deny your claim or legal defense based on lack of coverage, and your own adjuster must clarify the issues for you.

Workers' compensation insurance is required by law for Association employees. If the Association owns any vehicles or requires management to use them, automobile insurance may be necessary or required by law.

Also, the Association will want to seriously consider Directors and Officers liability insurance to protect directors and officers individually against liability from suits brought by third parties or even by members of the Association. Recruiting Board members is easier if they know that they are given the protection of this kind of insurance.

When buying any kind of insurance, you are faced with making decisions based upon costs that are determined by amounts of policy limits and deductibles, as well as the needs of the Association and its individual owners. These are reasons for you and your Association to rely on the work of experts—especially an insurance broker or agent.

Finally, it would be very wise to perform an annual review of the Association's insurance needs and coverages with an expert and to require management to do the same. The Association's Board will be doing its job by performing such annual reviews, along with other financially and legally important aspects of the Association's business.

Depending upon the geographical location of the community, there may be very important exclusions in the policies regarding earthquake, flood, or wind damage claims. Special wind damage or flood water insurance pools have been established for such property losses, and the insurance expert should be able to advise the Board as to what options it has in terms of protection and price.

Insurance is a method of indemnifying an insured for a loss. Another means of indemnification is by a *bond*. The most common types are *construction* and *fidelity* bonds. The former is vital if you or the Association are involved in any construction. Such bonds indemnify for performance, the quality of the work, or completion when a contractor walks off the job. A fidelity bond indemnifies the insured or beneficiary from loss caused by embezzlement, employee dishonesty, and similar losses caused by employees. Even independent contractors may be *special employees* for bonding purposes. Therefore, make sure that management companies and their employees, Association personnel who handle money, and anyone else who is to be entrusted with money is covered by a fidelity bond. This may be called a *blanket bond*, which covers all who fit a specified employment description.

Under no circumstances should you be afraid or shy about asking the insurance agent or broker to explain things carefully until you really understand them. Some people are better than others at explaining things. Remember, it is your home you are talking about.

# DUE PROCESS

The foundation of our legal system is the Constitution of the United States. Its most basic element is the idea of fundamental fairness. Due process ensures that fundamental fairness occurs.

Examples of due process are the right to an open hearing of charges and controversies, the right to confront and cross-examine accusers, the right to present evidence, and the right to a fair and impartial tribunal.

On a governmental level, the *executive branch* carries out and enforces laws enacted by the legislature and court decisions. The *legislative branch* enacts laws that apply to general problems that need solving or correcting. The *judicial branch* applies the laws to each specific case. Each case is unique and requires that the general law be applied to a unique situation. That explains why courts must have discretion given to them and why seemingly similar cases have different results. These same principles apply to Community Associations. Each Community Association is like a democracy, and fundamental fairness is therefore required.

In terms of a Homeowners Association, management is the executive branch, the Board is the legislature, and binding arbitration or court proceedings resolve matters if no settlement is reached, similar to the judicial branch. Yet there are matters handled by the Association that are judicial in nature and require due process, such as rule violation and delinquent payments.

The Association's governing documents provide for the resolution of a violation of its rules. Who shall hold the hearings and how they are conducted may also be provided for in the governing documents. The Board is responsible for making sure that proper notice and fair treatment are given in the enforcement of Association rules.

Due process extends to the treatment of Board members and owners at meetings. The Board may not run roughshod over the rights of those who have a right to speak. Generally, the Bylaws establish the rules by which all meetings are governed. They are usually from *Robert's Rules of Order*, and are structured to provide fundamental fairness in the conduct of Board and Committee meetings.

Minority rights are protected, but a recalcitrant minority, such as a disruptive owner, cannot control or thwart a meeting and the majority decision. If such an owner or group of owners tries to obstruct meetings, the President may entertain a motion to act on the subject at hand. If it is seconded and voted upon, that ends the subject. If the obstruction continues, the President can temporarily recess the meeting and if things get completely out of hand, a motion to adjourn, if carried, may solve the problem. An adjournment to a later date—or even a later time on the same day—can often help to defuse a volatile situation.

The proper use of parliamentary procedure provided for in *Robert's Rules of Order* can help greatly in keeping meetings civil and productive.

## ENFORCEMENT

Enforcing Community Association rules can be the most difficult aspect of living in the Community. Each Community is unique, and enforcement must be tailored to fit each Community's governing documents and special characteristics.

Unless the governing documents state otherwise, the Board has the duty to enforce the Association's rules. Enforcement begins with some kind of violation. The Board may establish a Committee to deal with violations or with certain kinds of violations. The Board would then act on the recommendations of the Committee.

Such violations may be reported actively by the Association security personnel or as a result of inspections by management. Violations may also be reported passively by other owners or governmental agencies. Whether or not the Association goes out looking for violations or waits for them to come to it, when a violation is reported, it must be clearly defined and accurately documented in a written report.

Once management is aware of a reported violation, and determines that it is a true violation and not just a spiteful complaint, the Board must begin proceeding immediately to conduct a hearing. All enforcement proceedings must have the following as part of their foundation:

- ◆ clear and unequivocal written complaint;
- ◆ immediate notice to the offending party of the violation;

- ◆ offer to allow a reasonable time, if appropriate, to remedy the violation;
- ◆ offer to mediate the matter;
- ◆ notice of a speedy and fair hearing date if the remedy is not made or if mediation fails; and,
- ◆ notice of the potential fine or other enforcement method that the violation requires.

If this list looks a lot like due process to you, you are right. There is no area more in need of due process than in rules enforcement.

The rules must be enforced equally—that means no special treatment must be shown to any owner. They must be enforced immediately to avoid the risk that other owners might get the impression that they can get away with violating the rules, too. The Board does not want a revolution on its hands. The very heart of Community living must be reinforced by having all of the owners aware that due process is afforded to the violating owner.

Beware of the Board member, manager, or owner who wants to strictly enforce everything that seems to be violated. Overzealousness is the potential enemy of harmony in the Community.

The Board must operate the Association as a business and exercise its best judgment in fulfilling its fiduciary duty to the owners. Boards vary from year to year, so each Board must familiarize itself with policies of preceding Boards and not vary from them drastically without public hearings or Committee meetings. This will give the Board the opportunity to hear from the owners and give the owners the satisfaction that they are participating in the process. More importantly, the owners receive notice so that future violations and resulting enforcement are dealt with using due process.

Enforcement may be accomplished by court proceedings and fines. Injunctive relief is a common way of enforcing rules of a substantial nature. Such relief is obtained when a court is petitioned to issue an injunction mandating or prohibiting something, and the petition is granted.

Any court procedure is expensive because of the complex nature of such procedures and the need for lawyers. As discussed in the next chapter, mediation is a less expensive way of problem resolution than litigation.

The most troublesome form of resolution is inaction. The problems of rules violations rarely go away. They multiply, because laxity on the part of the Board becomes immediately apparent to owners. The owners will be motivated to violate the rules to suit themselves, expecting no enforcement against them. Inequity and chaos will result. Allowing a violation to be continued and unenforced "just for this case" is just another form of inaction—creating more problems for the Association.

Finally, if enforcement is carried out, a reasonable time must be given for compliance. That is also part of the due process given to owners in all of the enforcement proceedings.

## CONFLICTS OF INTEREST

A *conflict of interest* interferes with the ability to fulfill a duty to one entity because of a duty to another. As a Board member for your Community Association, your duty is to the well-being of the Association—and not your personal gain.

For example, you may feel strongly that the hallway carpeting needs to be replaced as economically as possible. If you own a carpeting company, naturally you have a duty to maximize your company's profits. If your firm is put forth—by you or someone else—as a source for the new floor covering, your duties to the two entities are in conflict. If you are a Board member, you have a conflict of interest. In such a case, you should withdraw your company's name to avoid the conflict.

Not all conflicts of interest are this clear-cut. They typically revolve around matters of money, gifts, rules, and confidentiality. In each case, your duties of care, confidentiality, and fiduciary responsibility to your Association are challenged by the temptation to breach those duties in the interest of another party. As in the carpet example, the other party that interferes with your duty to the Association's interests could in fact be you—your business or personal interests. Equally, the other party could be a family member, friend, neighbor, professional associate, business, or organization in which you have an interest. Whomever the parties and whatever the issues, in conflicts of interest there often arises the temptation to exert influence to bend the rules or to reveal information that would compromise the confidentiality of the Association and its members.

An Association's Directors or managers have a responsibility to identify and disclose any conflicts of interest that affect their ability to perform a job responsibility. In some cases, a conflict of interest could be managed by abstaining from discussions or votes on the issue under consideration.

In all cases, a conflict of interest should be identified, revealed, and dealt with immediately. The notion that it will go away or no one will ever know is rarely true and never productive. The failure to disclose conflicts is a disservice to both entities, and will sooner or later lead to embarrassment for all parties. A written waiver of conflict may cure these problems. (Any waiver should be discussed with independent legal advice.) Nevertheless, even this should be avoided.

Human behavior involves the close relationship between individuals. This is true in Community Associations, creating perhaps even more closeness because of the strong identification with a home living space.

Owners, Board members, and managers naturally develop friendships with each other, and small favors are going to pass among them. These cannot be helped and are probably a positive influence on healthy relationships.

However, when such things bring about a detriment to others or cause a negative financial impact on the Association, then such a conflict must be prevented or terminated immediately. An often overlooked example of this kind of situation is the formation of cliques within an Association. To say that cliques are bad is to oversimplify the situation, but it is true that bad cliques are bad for the Association.

Close associations of people with similar interests is a natural phenomenon in human relationships. They will happen as a part of normal human behavior. In fact, they are probably a necessary part of the health and growth of Community Associations.

However, a group or clique that controls a Board may choose to do things that are bad for the entire Association. If the clique is controlled by management, the power of management is out of proportion, and the likelihood of corruption is increased. Preferential treatment for vendors, the failure of competitive bidding, and outright cash kickbacks involving managers and Board members can result.

The normal business of living in an Association, as in any other lifestyle, involves the inevitable conflicts of life. No one needs the destructive effects of conflicts of interest to aggravate them even further.

Exposing such conflicts immediately, discussing them in open meetings, and actively seeking legal advice for the Association can help eliminate such conflicts before they create the disasters that can bring about the insolvency or even bankruptcy of an Association.

Ultimately, if the Board and management are diligent in following, enforcing, and amending the governing documents—and work in conjunction with their attorney and insurance advisors—the Association can be protected. This will prevent many legal problems from occurring and will control the impact from those issues that do escalate.

# –5–
# RESOLVING CONFLICTS

It is quite understandable that people are going to have conflicts with each other—especially in an Association involving their homes. Conflict is one of the basic characteristics of being human. Successful human endeavors are those in which conflicts are resolved with leadership and the participation of all sides. Essentially, the important element in such success is the feeling that each participant has of being treated fairly.

Some people feel that fairness is getting everything their way. They can become the troublemakers that an Association needs to deal with occasionally. This is all the more reason to have prescribed resolution procedures in place, as well as enforcement when that becomes necessary. Skillful managers and Boards can minimize the use of these procedures in most instances—especially enforcement—by diplomacy and negotiation.

## NEGOTIATING WITHIN THE COMMUNITY ASSOCIATION

A Community Association must be run as a business, and as in any business, conflict and compromise are an inevitable part of the day-to-day management. When conflicts arise in the relationships between Board members, management, or the Association members, successful negotiations can lead to satisfactory solutions.

Formal negotiations are governed by the Association's controlling documents, such as the CC&Rs and Bylaws. Local legislation may further define your options. Some states call for offering the option of *alternative dispute resolution* (ADR), such as mediation or arbitration, before a lawsuit is filed. Because of the great expense and time-consuming nature of court litigation, alternatives have a growing popularity.

Regardless of a person's ethnic, cultural, religious, or social background, conflicts between people are going to arise. Naturally, certain religious or cultural customs can create unique conflicts. Even when the community consists of people from the same background, conflicts will occur. Within the confines of a Community Association, an optimum way in which these conflicts can be resolved includes internal dispute resolution.

*Internal dispute resolution* (IDR) can be involved in two situations—first, when the dispute is between owners only, and second, when the dispute is between owners and the Association. The first kind can escalate into the second kind if management is brought in. Some jurisdictions have statutory provisions for dispute resolution, which set out formal procedures, including prerequisites for dispute resolution, before very expensive litigation is involved.

Unless the subject matter of the conflicts is of such major proportion that management must be brought in immediately, the first step is usually a phone call or personal conversation to deal with the problem. If this approach does not resolve the issue, then a written note or letter is suggested.

If the written approach is unsuccessful, then a letter to the Association management, accompanied by a copy of the note or letter sent previously, is suggested to bring others into the resolution process. With management involved in the dispute, mediation can be utilized in an informal or formal way to solve the problem, with the parties bearing the expenses equally.

Management may want to try to help negotiate a settlement informally. However, care must be exercised, because some owners may perceive that management is taking sides, and a troubling situation may become worse or turn into a prolonged problem. By trying to resolve problems internally and not involving management at first, most owners solve their problems and forge connections with neighbors that otherwise might not have happened.

In a Community Association, issues can become very personal and even emotional. Strong feelings can interfere with successful communication. Matters are only worsened if neighbors are forced into litigation.

## Guidelines for Negotiation

Professional help through mediation may save a great deal of expense and vexation. A few guidelines for negotiating can be helpful in any conflict.

- Have all of the relevant facts before entering the process. Do your homework. Consider your position carefully, and consider your opponent's position and points of contention.
- Successful negotiation involves compromise on the part of all of the parties. Determine how much you are willing to concede. Know the limits of your position—legal, financial, and emotional.
- Enter the process with an open mind. Unrealistic expectations, take-it-or-leave-it offers, lack of preparation, and strident adversarial attitudes doom negotiations before they begin. If you are unable to contain your emotions on the issue being negotiated, consider appointing someone to represent your position in your stead.
- Listen. You may wish to set ground rules for the length of time each speaker can hold the floor. When someone is speaking, give your full attention.
- Make a determined effort to be aware of others' feelings. Put yourself in their positions and imagine how you would feel and react.
- Maintain a pleasant demeanor. Overly aggressive advocacy has its place, but not in negotiation or mediation. You should maintain a strong position, but not an oppressive one.
- If possible, let your opponent make the opening offer. If you must make the first offer, it should:
    - send a signal that you are interested in resolving the problem by being reasonable;

- ◆ give the other side something to think about, but leave you room for alternative offers later; and,
- ◆ contain additional points that you are willing to concede, depending on the counteroffer.
- ◆ Maintain a strong position. If you give up too soon, you are likely to lose to those more tenacious than you. Always have a counterproposal to keep the dialogue going and to prevent the premature termination of negotiations. Always keep the door open.

Successful negotiations will probably lead to an agreement in which each side has conceded something. You may have given up something that was important to you, but by participating in negotiations, you also saved yourself and your Association time, headaches, and enormous financial resources.

Keep in mind the limitations on managers and owners. Neither can negotiate the terms of the CC&Rs or Bylaws. Neither can make exceptions to them—not even the Board can do so.

# MEDIATION

*Mediation* is simply defined as impartial third-party-assisted negotiation. A mediator may or may not be a lawyer, but may be anyone the parties trust who has the skills of a master negotiator. Each of the guidelines for negotiation previously mentioned applies to mediation as well.

For example, if cooking odors from a condominium are bothersome to a neighbor, and a phone call or letter has not been successful in solving the problem, mediation may be the solution. Perhaps the common airspace needs a separation wall to seal off the odors. This would involve the Association in the mediation because common areas are involved, and the expenses may be apportioned in negotiated amounts among the two owners and the Association.

Mediation is the method of choice to resolve disputes. Mediation is a process in which a mediator guides the parties through a settlement of their own case. It can be initiated at any stage of the proceedings, interrupted, and resumed at any time. All sides generally benefit from mediation.

Good mediators are difficult to find, but legal counsel experienced in Community Association law make it a point to find them. Since the mediator does not make decisions (only the parties do that), there is very little difficulty stemming from conflicts of interest or collusions—which can happen sometimes in arbitration. Most of the time, a successful mediation results in all sides feeling quite satisfied with the result.

Mediators can be facilitative or evaluative. An *evaluative mediator* injects opinions and evaluations in the proceedings, whereas a *facilitative mediator* does not. Both lead the parties toward resolving the disputes themselves. Sometimes in a business context, this is an amicable renegotiation of the deal. It is usually much more economical than any other dispute resolution format. To participate in mediation, it is necessary to include the people who make the final decision, as well as those who have critical knowledge of the matters in dispute. A positive tone must be maintained by all parties. If mediation does not work, you may have to go to arbitration or trial.

Mediation is completely different from arbitration. The mediator takes no evidence in a formal proceeding and makes no award or other formal decision. The parties and their lawyers resolve their dispute. Nonbinding arbitration frequently evolves into mediation, so you are best advised to choose mediation from the outset and avoid the great waste of time that nonbinding arbitration can become.

After a successful mediation, the parties should enter into a written agreement immediately, which includes all the agreed-upon terms. This is a contract and can be enforced.

Mediation is the most affordable and successful form of ADR. Of the three formats of dispute resolution—mediation, arbitration, and court proceedings—the latter two are litigation. A pleading must be filed and then an answer filed. An evidentiary hearing is held and a written decision is made. One side wins and the other side loses.

On the other hand, negotiation or mediation between the parties is not litigation. They both may occur during litigation, but not necessarily. In places where an arbitration award can be confirmed as a judgment, successful mediation can, by written stipulation, be deemed to be a binding arbitration. The agreement can be made, an award can be signed by the former mediator—now arbitrator—and it can all be confirmed in a court proceeding. This kind of procedure satisfies the claimant that the security of a judgment is available. It ends the conflict in the same way as any binding arbitration.

A stipulation for judgment may also be entered into for the purpose of setting up a payment schedule. If there is a default, then the entire amount is entered as a judgment. This can also be the award, after the mediation and the stipulation to binding arbitration.

These options can be agreed upon after the mediation. There need not even be any suit on file, or it can be done as the jury is deliberating after a trial. There is a great deal of flexibility for all parties. All parties usually pay the mediator equally, which motivates everyone to move the process along.

## ARBITRATION

There is no settlement in an *arbitration*. The arbitration results in an award. It is enforceable only by the written terms of the arbitration agreement or by the procedures of the local jurisdiction. Generally, this latter process confirms the award as a judgment by petitioning the court for such a confirmation.

When the petition is granted, the award is ordered to be entered as a judgment. After that is done, then the ultimate enforcement of execution on the judgment is available, and bank accounts and other properties can be attached.

Court proceedings, such as trials, defaults, and any other terminal proceedings, result in a judgment. This final result is the primary way to attach property or execute on the judgment and bring disputes to a close.

Binding arbitration is true litigation, although the rules of evidence may be relaxed. As in a trial, someone has to lose. In many jurisdictions, there is no appeal from an arbitration award—even if the arbitrators are wrong on the law or even the facts. In those jurisdictions, arbitration is a very harsh remedy—particularly when a contract calls for arbitration in situations where one party is in a weaker bargaining position and cannot avoid such an agreement for arbitration.

Arbitration may be very expensive because of lawyers' fees and expert witnesses, although costs are usually less than court proceedings. There may be either a single arbitrator or a panel of three arbitrators, and their expenses are shared equally by the parties. Having an uneven number of arbitrators assists both in speeding the process and in avoiding deadlocks.

The arbitrators hear evidence and make an award. The advantage is that the process is fast, fair, and final. A disadvantage is that appeal is unavailable, except for fraud or collusion by the arbitrators.

Another advantage of arbitration is that it can be held at times and in a place that is comfortable and convenient for the parties and witnesses.

Testimony under oath is required in arbitration, although there may be no written record of the proceedings. This has a sobering effect on most witnesses, and motivates many people to negotiate their dispute.

The recovery of attorney's fees, which can be considerable, also motivates the parties to negotiate a resolution. Such a recovery also suggests a way of handling the disruptive homeowner who has many vexing complaints. If the Association opts for arbitration for each such petty claim, the disruptive homeowner's prospect of having to pay both lawyers' fees if he or she loses can inhibit many such complaints.

The cooking odor example previously given demonstrates that a matter may not have to be tried or arbitrated. If that situation were arbitrated instead of resolved through mediation, the expenses and fees of three attorneys and the cost of arbitration would have to be paid by the owner who loses in the award to the winning owner.

The selection of arbitrators may take different forms, but the usual one is that each side selects an arbitrator, and the two appointees then select the third arbitrator. If there is only one arbitrator to be used and the parties cannot agree upon one, the court will appoint one upon the submission of a proper petition. The same applies to the third arbitrator if there is no agreement.

The parties pay the arbitrators equally. That expense, even for one arbitrator, plus one's own counsel fees, can really add up. If the agreement calls for payment of counsel fees to the prevailing party, then arbitration can be prohibitively expensive.

There are other forms of dispute resolution, such as early neutral evaluation and summary trials, in which only the basic elements of a case are argued before a judge or jury. The most effective options in Community Association disputes, however, are mediation and arbitration.

It has been suggested that each set of CC&Rs should require mandatory mediation of a disputed matter for a minimum of three hours or until the matter is resolved, and then binding arbitration or court proceedings if the question is not resolved. However, binding arbitration can be expensive, and therefore abused by some Boards.

If the Board wants to punish someone by abusing the use of arbitration to resolve every little dispute (some of which may be contrived), such an abused owner may have to resort to the court for protection and seek damages from the Association.

Although arbitration is a very good way to resolve disputes, the expense is often about the same as serious mediation. The secret to successful dispute resolution of any kind in any format—from court trial to mediation—is thorough preparation. Such a process motivates the parties to study their files and evaluate them. This enables negotiation to occur much more easily. The sooner the preparation begins, the sooner the negotiations begin.

Legal counsel for the Association must be accountable for what it is doing for the case or cases it is handling. Reports to the Board must be required on a regular basis. Even if it adds to the expense when the fee is hourly, it is probably worth it. The lawyers are motivated to be thoroughly familiar with the file, thus making settlement a reality sooner rather than later. As in all disputes, litigation should be the last resort. This includes arbitration.

## DISPUTE RESOLUTION DIAGRAM

This diagram shows the five most common techniques used to settle or close a matter. The arrows show clockwise motion as a conflict moves toward resolution. It is clear that expenses and time increase as each technique must be used.

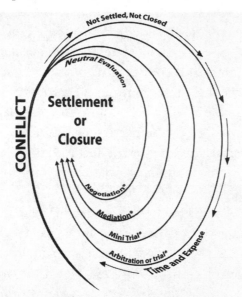

Not Settled, Not Closed

Neutral Evaluation

CONFLICT

**Settlement**
**or**
**Closure**

Negotiation*

Mediation*

Mini Trial*

Arbitration or trial*

Time and Expense

**\* Each of the preceding techniques**
**may be used simultaneously with the one below it.**

Settling a matter occurs when the parties agree on the terms and it is then resolved. Closing a matter occurs when the complaining party withdraws the complaint and the matter is closed. The exception is when a complaint is taken to mediation, arbitration, or trial. In that case, costs and fees may have been incurred that the withdrawing party may have to pay, according to the terms of the agreement out of which the mediation or arbitration grew. The court may also order costs and fees incurred in a trial or mini trial up to the complaint's withdrawal.

The differences between the six most common dispute resolution techniques are quite clear.

1. In *neutral evaluation* (NE), the parties may be aided by having a more objective examination of all sides of a conflict. This may be done by one person or a group of people who are experts in a field such as construction, patents, labor law, or personal injury. A private or mock jury may give a verdict after hearing evidence that will later be presented to a real jury. The

private jurors can give valuable and neutral evaluation of witnesses, facts, theories, or issues. Neutral evaluation may be used in one of two ways. First, a party may have such an evaluation to help in negotiation, mediation, arbitration, or trial. Second, the parties may stipulate that the conclusions of an NE become the final settlement of the matter.

2. *Negotiation* is the most commonly used dispute resolution technique, because we do it many times a day with those around us. It is done by the parties involved and is binding only when the parties agree upon the result. It is a process that has been going on for thousands of years.

3. *Mediation* is impartial, third-party-assisted negotiation, and involves all of the aspects of negotiation, with the addition of impartial guidance to achieve a resolution more quickly and efficiently. This is especially true in complex and difficult cases.

4. *Mini trials* involve stipulation by the parties to certain evidence and issues, leaving only certain issues to be decided by the court or jury. Many times the issue of damages only will be tried by mini trial after a stipulation as to liability has been made. This saves a great deal of time and money. A jury of less than twelve may be used and a simple majority vote may be stipulated. Deposition transcripts and videos may be used instead of live testimony.

5. *Arbitration* is adversarial, and it is real litigation, even though the rules of evidence may be relaxed. The process is fast and may be done at times most convenient to the parties. There usually is no transcript and no right to appeal.

6. *Trial* is the most formal technique for resolving disputes, and is also the most expensive and time-consuming. There is a right to appeal, but that is also a very expensive process. A jury may be used, and one person has no way of avoiding it if the other party wants one. The very unpredictability of verdicts encourages settlements. As in arbitration, the parties have no direct involvement in the outcome, and strangers to the parties and the facts must make tough decisions about very important issues in the parties' lives.

# UNOFFENSIVE CORRESPONDENCE

Although all correspondence does not necessarily have within it legal considerations, much of what is sent by an Association may. An example is a notice that the owner's Association dues, fees, or assessments are delinquent. This is a common situation that calls for a letter from management. It is a circumstance in which the owner is probably under stress already—that is why there is a delinquency—and does not need to have the aggravation of a harsh, rude, cruel, unbusinesslike letter from management. Such a letter makes things worse for everyone.

The recipient of such a negative letter may be on the Board someday and have the power to change managers or management companies, or at least call for a management audit. All of those things can be avoided if the Board sets sensible policy guidelines for correspondence.

The following are some simple, general guidelines for correspondence with owners.

- ◆ Begin each paragraph with positive words, such as "thank you," "fortunately," "hopefully," "thankfully," "happily," "you," "your," and "please."
- ◆ Do not begin paragraphs with the words "I," "we," "our," "unfortunately," "regrettably," or any other words having a negative or egotistical connotation.
- ◆ Use short paragraphs containing no more than three sentences.
- ◆ Use long paragraphs only to bury bad news, and put the bad news in the middle of the paragraph.
- ◆ Begin and end a letter with an upbeat or positive sentence, if possible.
- ◆ Show that a copy of the letter is sent to a relevant party to underscore accountability and that someone else is involved, such as a Committee of the Board, the accountant, or legal counsel.

Some sample letters follow as suggestions for use, with modifications applicable for your Association. Although they are samples for use within the Association, the previously stated guidelines are applicable to all business correspondence with vendors, governmental agencies, publications, or other businesses or individuals.

With good leadership by management and the Board, and the participation of the interested owner members, a Community Association is able to get closer to the ideal of being a harmonious and fulfilling place to live.

## SAMPLE NOTICES, LETTERS, AND FORMS

A key to the success of the Association—legally and operationally— is to ensure that written notice is provided to homeowners whenever appropriate. Letters and notices should be straightforward and timely. Those who receive them should understand why the letter or notice was sent and what they are to do in response.

By the time an issue requires a letter from the Association to a homeowner, there is usually a problem at hand. That does not mean, however, that the letters can or should be rude. In fact, it works against the Board, the management, and the Association if the letters are anything but professional.

The following letters are samples of the correspondence that might be used by an Association for typical problems or issues that arise. They can be adapted to fit any Association's needs—but what is most important is that the tone remains the same.

Following the letters are standardized meeting notices that can be used to announce upcoming Board, Committee, and other meetings. Again, consistency is the key. The information should be direct and easy to read, so that homeowners know exactly why, when, and where the meeting is being held, and what is to be on the agenda. This way, homeowners who wish to attend can do so and be prepared with any questions or concerns that might apply.

In addition, samples of a number of useful forms are provided to facilitate communications and recordkeeping for the Association.

Two major goals are accomplished simply by ensuring that the Association's documentation is clear and consistent. First, it helps protect the Association and its homeowners in case any situation escalates to litigation. After all, the courts will want to be assured that the Association was clear in its expectations and demands. Second, well-written letters and notices ensure that the sense of community that is so important to a successful living situation is protected and preserved. Taking the time to review and edit written communication can only help the Community and everyone who lives there.

## Table of Letters, Notices, and Forms

## Sample Letter One
## Letter from Owner to Owner


Date: _____

From: _____, Unit \_\_\_\_\_

To: _____, Unit \_\_\_\_\_

Dear _____:

This refers to our conversation of _____ [date] about the problem of _____
_____.

Please understand that this is a request that we resolve the problem, without time-consuming formalities. Let me know your suggestions for a solution to the problem, as I prefer not to involve management if at all possible.

Sincerely,

**Sample Letter Two**
**Letter from Owner to Owner with a Copy to Management**

Date: _____

Subject: _____

Dear _____:

This is regarding the problem that we have discussed.

Hopefully, it can soon be resolved amicably. By sending a copy of this letter to management, along with a copy of my letter to you dated _____, I am requesting that all of us meet to resolve the problem without a great deal of expense.

On _____ [date] or _____ [date] I am available to have such a meeting at _____ _____ [manager's office or site of problem] or wherever is convenient for you. Please get back to me before _____ [date/time] if there is a date agreeable to you.

Sincerely,

cc: _____, Manager

**Sample Letter Three**
**Delinquency Letter**

Date: _____

Re: Delinquent _____

Dear _____:

Please take this as notification that your payments for _____ have not been made, according to our records.

You are reminded that under Section _____ of the _____ [governing document name] of the Association, all payments for _____ are to be made on or before the _____ day of the month.

Hopefully, this can be corrected to avoid the enforcement required under Section _____ of the _____ [governing document name].

Thank you for your kind attention to this matter as soon as possible.

Sincerely,


_____
Manager

## Sample Letter Four
## Violation of Rules

Date: _____

Re: Rule _____

Dear _____:

This is to notify you that there are complaints that _____ _____ [loud noises, odors, etc.] have been reported coming from your property in violation of Section _____ of the Association _____ [governing document name].

Please contact us as soon as possible so that we can verify the accuracy of these complaints and make corrections immediately, if necessary.

Thank you for helping all of us to maintain the high standards we want for _____ [Association name].

Sincerely,

_____

Manager

cc: Board of Directors

**Sample Letter Five**
**Parking Violation**

Date: _____

Re: Parking Violation _____

This is posted on your vehicle to notify you that this parking space is for _____ [residents, loading, handicapped] and is not permitted for your vehicle. A copy of this notice is retained in the management office and if your vehicle is not removed by _____ [date/time], it will be towed away in accordance with Section _____ of _____ [governing document name].

Thank you for your cooperation in keeping _____ _____ [name of Association] a pleasant place for community living.

_____
Management

and

_____
Security

cc: Board of Directors

## Sample Letter Six
## Foreclosure Letter

Date: _____

Re: Delinquent Assessments

Dear _____:

Please take this as notification that your payments of assessments have not been made according to our records for ___ months.

You are reminded that under Section _____ of the _____ _____ [governing document name] of the Association, all payments for _____ [name of Association] are to be made, and if delinquent, foreclosure proceedings may be initiated.

Please also take this as notification that this initiates the foreclosure process.

Thank you for your kind attention to this matter as soon as possible.

Sincerely,

_____

Manager

**Sample Notice One**
**Annual Membership Meeting**

_____ HOMEOWNERS ASSOCIATION
NOTICE OF ANNUAL MEMBERSHIP MEETING

Notice is hereby given that the Annual Meeting of the _____
_____ Homeowners Association will be held on
_____ [date] at _____ [time].

AGENDA
       Open Meeting: _____
       Election of Directors: _____
       Other Balloting (if any): _____
       Annual Report: _____
       Directors Elect Officers: _____
       Close Meeting: _____

There will be a vote of the membership on the election of Board
members.

Members who will be unable to attend the meeting should execute
the enclosed proxy and return it to the _____
_____ [name and address of individual in charge of collecting proxies] by _____ [date].

The meeting will be held at the _____ [name of
facility], located at _____ [address].

The Board of Directors
_____ Homeowners Association

**Sample Notice Two**
**Regular Board of Directors Meeting**

_____ HOMEOWNERS ASSOCIATION
NOTICE OF REGULAR BOARD OF DIRECTORS MEETING

Notice is hereby given that the regular meeting of the Board of Directors for the _____ Homeowners Association will be held on _____ [date] at _____ [time].

AGENDA
    Open Meeting: _____

    Approval of Minutes: _____

    Reports: _____

    Old Business: _____

    New Business: _____

    Close Meeting: _____

The meeting will be held at the _____ [name of facility], located at _____ [address].

The Board of Directors
_____ Homeowners Association

**Sample Notice Three**
**Special Board of Directors Meeting**


_____ HOMEOWNERS ASSOCIATION
NOTICE OF SPECIAL BOARD OF DIRECTORS MEETING


Notice is hereby given that a special meeting of the Board of Directors for the _____ Homeowners Association will be held on _____ [date] at _____ [time].


AGENDA
     Open Meeting: _____
     Approval of Minutes: _____
     Reports: _____
     Old Business: _____
     New Business: _____
     Close Meeting: _____

The meeting will be held at the _____ [name of facility], located at _____ [address].


The Board of Directors
_____ Homeowners Association

**Sample Notice Four**
**Executive Session Board Meeting**

_____ HOMEOWNERS ASSOCIATION
NOTICE OF EXECUTIVE SESSION BOARD MEETING

Notice is hereby given that an Executive Session of the Board of Directors for the _____ Homeowners Association will be held on_____ [date] at _____ [time].

AGENDA
     Open Meeting: _____
     Approval of Minutes: _____
     Reports: _____
     Old Business: _____
     New Business: _____
     Close Meeting: _____

The meeting will be held at the _____ [name of facility], located at _____ [address].

The Board of Directors
_____ Homeowners Association

**Sample Form One**
**General Request and Review Form**

## GENERAL REQUEST AND REVIEW FORM

Name _____ Date _____

Address or unit _____
Phone _____

Nature of request (please be as specific as possible): _____
_____
_____
_____
_____

- - - - - - - - - - - - - - - - - - - - - - - - - - - - - - - - - - - - - - - - - - -

### For Office Use Only

Date received in management office _____
Inspected on _____ By _____
Approved on _____ By _____
Reason for disapproval _____
_____
_____

Owner notified of decision on _____ By _____

## Sample Form Two
## Architectural Request and Review Form

### ARCHITECTURAL REQUEST AND REVIEW FORM

Name _____ Date _____

Address or unit _____
Phone _____

Nature of request (please be as specific as possible and attach a sketch showing location and dimensions): _____
_____
_____
_____
_____

- - - - - - - - - - - - - - - - - - - - - - - - - - - - - - - - - - - - - - - - - - - - - - - -

### For Office Use Only

Date submitted to Committee _____
Date received in management office _____
Inspected on _____ By _____
Approved on _____ By _____
Reason for disapproval _____
_____
_____
_____

Owner notified of decision on _____ By _____

**Sample Form Three**
**Emergency Contact List**

## EMERGENCY CONTACT LIST
_____ [name of complex or Association]

[Your Association emergency contact list should be prepared and maintained on a computer so that it can be updated easily. Following is a list of people and services that you may want to include. For each one, include a contact name, daytime phone number, and after-hours phone or pager (if appropriate). Date the form so that newer versions are easily distinguished from older ones.]

This list is provided for your convenience. Please be aware that you may incur costs associated with calls placed to these services, depending upon the location and nature of your request. All non-emergency problems should be directed to the manager.

Fire/Police/Ambulance Emergencies—911

Board of directors
Association employees
    Accountant            Insurance agent
    Attorney              Management company

Service contractors
    Antennae             Pest control
    Cleaning service     Plumber
    Electrician           Roofer
    Elevator             Security service
    Gardener            Security system
    Glass                 Snow removal
    HVAC                 Street lighting
    Landscaping        Trash removal
    Locksmith           Other
    Painter

Fire, nonemergency

Police, nonemergency

## Sample Form Four
## Manager's Log of Owners' Requests

## MANAGER'S LOG OF OWNERS' REQUESTS

| Date | Time | Owner's Name | Unit | Address | Phone | Description of Request | Disposition | Completed |
|------|------|--------------|------|---------|-------|------------------------|-------------|-----------|
|      |      |              |      |         |       |                        |             |           |
|      |      |              |      |         |       |                        |             |           |
|      |      |              |      |         |       |                        |             |           |
|      |      |              |      |         |       |                        |             |           |
|      |      |              |      |         |       |                        |             |           |
|      |      |              |      |         |       |                        |             |           |
|      |      |              |      |         |       |                        |             |           |
|      |      |              |      |         |       |                        |             |           |
|      |      |              |      |         |       |                        |             |           |
|      |      |              |      |         |       |                        |             |           |

## Sample Form Five
## Architectural Violation Log

# ARCHITECTURAL VIOLATION LOG

| Unit No. | Unit Owner | Description of Violation | Date Noted | Inspected | First Notice | Second Notice | Second Inspection | Attorney | Comments |
|---|---|---|---|---|---|---|---|---|---|
| | | | | | | | | | |
| | | | | | | | | | |
| | | | | | | | | | |
| | | | | | | | | | |
| | | | | | | | | | |
| | | | | | | | | | |
| | | | | | | | | | |
| | | | | | | | | | |
| | | | | | | | | | |
| | | | | | | | | | |

# –6–
# GROUND RULES FOR SUCCESS

Community Associations can only succeed if they are managed well—not just well-managed. This means that as you look at your Community and its needs, you need to observe how it is managed—not just by whom. What are the methods to track and monitor projects? How is information disseminated? Are there any current risks to the Community? Are those risks legal? Financial? Structural?

Throughout your research, you must ask yourself, *How do I know how my Community is doing?* The questions of how much you know and from where the information comes lie at the heart of making sure your Community and its Association are safe. Only then can you be sure that your investment and your home are safe.

What must you do to find out whether your Association is well-managed? It starts with ground rules.

Ground rules are the guidelines by which those who oversee the Community and its needs must operate to succeed. The ground rules are not the same as the CC&Rs or any other governing documents. They are the active commitments that each member of the managing bodies (i.e., the Board, Committees, and management) make to one another to ensure the success of the greater Community.

Organizations that succeed do so because they are consistent and predictable. Those people who are overseeing the organization and its activities not only know the ground rules, but they ensure that those rules are set and followed. That way, everybody knows what is expected of them and everybody else. It also ensures that anyone who is working against the rules—and, as such, the good of the Community—can be easily identified and appropriate action can be taken.

The Community's ground rules must be actively followed by the Board, Committees, and management. These rules act as much to provide role modeling as they do to create consistency throughout the Community. It does not matter whether you have an outside manager overseeing your Association's activities or if that responsibility is performed by a resident manager—the ground rules apply to everyone involved in the management of the Community.

## THE GROUND RULES

There are five basic ground rules that you and everyone involved in your Community's management and oversight must follow. Only by doing so can you ensure that the Association is managed well and well-managed. The five ground rules are:

1. be consistent;
2. be vigilant;
3. enforce all the rules;
4. review documents regularly; and,
5. ask when you do not know.

Depending upon your Association and its needs, you may decide to add some ground rules to the list. Some communities add ground rules such as *be honest; be respectful of others;* or, *ask, do not attack.* These and others should be added if they will help your Board, Committee members, and management do their jobs well.

The ground rules should be posted at every meeting. They should also be reviewed periodically to ensure that everyone understands them and how they apply to your Community. This is particularly important if you have new Board or Committee members, or a new manager joining the group. In that case, special time should be set aside to discuss the ground rules in detail, ask questions, and make sure that everybody understands them and recommits themselves to their enforcement.

The following sections detail each ground rule and how it applies to the Community and its Association. As you read the descriptions, think about how your Community operates right now. Look for opportunities for improvement. Think about how you might introduce your thoughts to your fellow Community members—whether Board or Committee members, management, or just your friends within the Community who also want to become involved in the betterment of their home, Community, and Association.

## Be Consistent

Consistency creates a sense of safety and comfort for all of those around us. Everybody knows what to expect, no matter what the circumstances. Decisions are the same—no matter who makes them. Consistency and a sense of safety are synonymous.

It is not just the CC&Rs or governing documents with which you must be consistent—although that is absolutely necessary. It is also the way that you deal with problems within the Community that makes consistency so important.

One of the more popular tricks that residents play is to pit one Board, Committee, or management member against the others. It is the idea that "if Mom says no, go ask Dad." That can only work if "Mom" and "Dad" are not consistent in the way that they make decisions. Rather than allowing residents to believe that they can ask one person and get the answer they want—knowing that they would not get the same answer from another person—it is the responsibility of all those in management to make sure that they are consistent with the rules and with each other.

Realistically, that is a very big task. It is hard enough for any individual to be consistent from situation to situation. Try to bring that consistency to a group and the difficulties in the early stages seem momentous. The best way to overcome those difficulties is to commit to working toward being consistent, and then, at each meeting, discuss decisions in the larger context. Were they consistent with other decisions being made? Are certain residents trying to play one person off another? What should be done to make sure that everyone is consistent from situation to situation?

Being consistent requires an objective look at how you are behaving from situation to situation—and adjusting your behaviors so there is no discernable difference from one set of circumstances to the next. Even though it seems as if every problem is separate and apart from all the others, that is not actually the case.

**EXAMPLE:** In one Community, one of the Board members was constantly complaining about residents who made any changes to the outside of their homes that might be seen by others. She bothered the manager, the other Board members, even the residents themselves—sometimes even insulting them for their lack of consideration for their neighbors and the overall value of the property.

Somehow, though, it never occurred to that same Board member that she had made changes to the outside of her residence that were breaking the same rules she was complaining about. For months she ignored the manager and other Board members as they mentioned, asked, and demanded that she bring her residence into compliance.

She truly did not see that it was the same thing. She was guilty of violating the same rules for which she was pointing a finger at others, yet she thought that, somehow, her situation was different, not because she was a Board member, but because she did not find her violation offensive—to her or to the value of the property. It was only everyone else's infractions that created a problem.

Once it was brought to her attention, she realized her mistake. Until that time, she did not see her inconsistency. Once she did, appropriate action was taken—by her and others—and the problems were solved.

### Be Vigilant

The best way to build upon consistency and ensure that ground rules are being observed is to be vigilant. It is so easy for the rules of the Association to be overlooked. There is a tendency to want to believe that this time was different, that the residents know better and will take it upon themselves to correct their behavior.

Perhaps the Board, Committee, or management members are just tired. They know that something is wrong and they even know that they must do something about it. But how many times must they take the same actions, for the same—or different—people, until everybody understands their responsibility to their Community and their Association?

They have every right to be tired. At the best of times, being vigilant is not easy. Add the responsibility of knowing that your decisions can make or break your Community and your own home, and it often seems the weight of the world is resting on your shoulders.

That being said, being vigilant—in combination with being consistent—lessens the weight of the world. Ultimately, it allows those who are overseeing the good of the Community to set and demonstrate standards for how the Community is going to work.

Vigilance in the management of the Community and its Association makes all of its operations more predictable. Most importantly, it becomes predictable that the Community is operating as it should and must for the best interests of all the residents.

**EXAMPLE:** In a townhome community there was a couple whose children invariably threw their candy and ice cream wrappers in the driveway and garage areas. Everybody knew the perpetrators. A number of residents spoke to the managing members of the Community, complaining about the mess and the fact that the parents disregarded the requests of the neighbors to teach their children to throw their garbage into the appropriate receptacles.

Because no action was being taken, other residents began breaking other rules. Their feeling—justified in their eyes—was that they and their children should not be held to a higher standard if no one was going to ensure that others were not held responsible. That part of the Community quickly began to look like a slum—with property values adjusting appropriately downward.

Finally, the Board members realized that they could not be nice about the rules of the Community. They had to be vigilant. What had started out as a single instance—something to be treated only as a minor problem—had escalated to a very real problem for the whole of the Community.

Action was taken. A meeting was held with the residents of that part of the Community. Cleanup teams were established to bring the common areas back to their previously pristine appearance. It was even decided by the residents of that area that a neighborhood watch program would be established, where residents would not only be on the lookout for potential criminals, but would also report on those children who violated the common area cleanliness rules. The problem never recurred.

The easiest way to bring vigilance to the management of the Association is for the Board, Committee, and management members to review the requirements of the Community. They must look at the need and rule requirements, and discuss which are most important, which are most frequently broken or ignored, and which have been most often passed over or excused—no matter what the reason.

Whether the requirements are aesthetic or operational (such as ensuring that ongoing preventive maintenance is performed), by going through this identification and discussion process, the managing members of the Community are able to identify where they need to put their attention and are then able to do so. Then, if necessary and appropriate, they can work with residents, management, or vendors who must address these problems to solve them and avoid recurrences. By being both vigilant and consistent—from requirement to requirement and person to person—the Community will operate in a much more predictable manner.

## Enforce All the Rules

The logical outgrowth of consistency and vigilance is that all rules of the Community and its Association are enforced. By committing to this action, the Board, Committees, and management are demonstrating their respect for the Association and all of its members—the residents of the Community. There can be no cherry-picking in rule enforcement. If the rule is not worth enforcing, then it should not be a rule. It is that simple.

No one likes to follow rules unless the rules are acceptable to them, no matter what the reason. If you allow Community members to follow the rules they like and ignore the rest, then you might as well have no rules at all.

Management is management. Whether it is the Board, Committees, a manager, or a management company, the responsibility of management is to ensure the health and well-being of the organization they oversee. It is a duty and responsibility that cannot be shirked.

No, it is not pleasant. Yes, it very often pits you against your neighbors. However, your responsibility is not to the individuals, but to the greater good of the Community. When you are dealing with problems in the Community, you are not dealing with individuals. It may be an individual perpetrator, but it is not an individual problem. The problem is one that affects the community as a whole.

If a rule does not make sense—and that often happens—change it. Go through the proper procedures and channels to have the rule reviewed, and altered or deleted. However, until that rule no longer exists or has been changed to reflect the new needs of the Community, it must be enforced as it is written.

One of the most common rule enforcement problems has to do with pets. Sometimes a Community is established that does not allow pets because the original residents had no interest in them. Over time, that may well have changed.

Of course, those who bought into the Community knew that pets were not allowed. However, maybe they were given a gift, or they were lonely and wanted an animal companion in their home. No matter the reason, the pet is now there and it opens the door for other homeowners to demand the same.

**EXAMPLE:** In one Community, a resident had a near terror of cats. Upon finding out that one of her neighbors had a cat in her condominium, she was convinced that there were wild animals wandering the halls. A simple house cat—neither large nor dangerous—suddenly took on the size and threat of a puma on the prowl. The resident loudly ensured that the Board and manager knew that the no-pet rule was being broken.

Ultimately, it was found out that a number of residents had cats, small dogs, and fish in their condominiums. The decision was made to review the no-pet rule. Eventually, it was overturned and pets were allowed. The vocal resident—while not pleased—adjusted to the new situation. Pets were to be kept in the condominiums and not allowed to wander the halls.

At least, she felt, there would be no more surprises. There were pets in the building, and either she would have to get used to them or move to another location. She is still happily living in her original condominium.

### Review Documents Regularly
All of this leads to the need to regularly review the governing and other documents of the Community. These documents are not cast in

concrete. They are living, breathing means of supporting the needs of the Community. As the needs of the Community change, so should its documents. The only way to know whether that must be done is to regularly review those documents for their applicability.

Sometimes you review the documents to make sure that everybody understands the same rules the same way. Very often one person believes that he or she knows what a particular rule says and he or she operates in keeping with that understanding. Invariably, that same person has taken the time and effort to explain the rule to all and sundry to ensure they understand why the rule is being enforced in a particular way. More often than not, that person's understanding of that rule is incorrect.

It is not that this person is intentionally biasing the rule in a particular direction. He or she may have no vested interest one way or the other. It is simply his or her understanding or misunderstanding of what the rule says.

The interpretation of the rules and regulations of the Community often come from people who are no longer on the Board or Committees, or in management. They may not even live in the Community any more. But once, long ago, one person told someone else about a particular rule and how it works, and over the course of time that is exactly what everybody learned to believe about the rule.

This is where owner manuals become crucial. By laying down the general rules of the Community for everyone to know and see, it is much easier for everybody to have a shared understanding and knowledge about the way the Community works. Beyond that, the Board, Committees, and management should plan an annual review of the various rules and regulations of the Community to ensure that they are understood the same way, are still timely, and are being enforced.

## Ask When You Do Not Know

One ground rule that makes all the others easy to follow is *ask when you do not know*. Whether the question is about the rules and regulations of the Community, how those rules and regulations are being enforced, the financials, the operations, or anything else, do not assume you know and understand everything. Do not assume every-body else understands everything either—they do not.

Every person throughout the Community has unique gifts of understanding. This is particularly true and important among those involved in the management and oversight of the Community and its Association. A good blend of varied expertise provides the greatest benefit to the Community.

People tend to focus in areas in which they are most comfortable. For example, you may find the following is the case in your Community.

- The President will be the most strategic member of the managing entities.
- The Vice President will be most comfortable as liaison between Board members.
- The Secretary will be the most detail-oriented person for nonfinancial operations.
- The Treasurer will be the person most comfortable with balance sheets and the financials of the Association.
- The manager will be the most comfortable and conversant with the operational needs of the Association and the Community.

Granted, this is an oversimplification, but it gives you the basic idea. Each person brings his or her own expertise to the management of the Association. As such, each person is a resource to the others and can provide information on an as-needed basis.

Vendors, whether attorneys and accountants or HVAC technicians and gardeners, are also available knowledge resources. If you need to know something, ask. Do not be embarrassed and do not think your question is stupid. Chances are, if you want to know, there is at least one other person in the group who would also like to know, but is afraid to ask. Not asking the question is a much greater risk to the Community than taking the time of others to get the knowledge that you all need to best manage your Community.

Remember, Communities must not only be well-managed, but managed well. By following the ground rules, you will find that you and your associates involved in the management and oversight of your Community and its Association will have a much easier time of it—now and in the future.

## THE DISRUPTIVE HOMEOWNER

In Community Association living, you may be forced to confront personalities and issues that you find disagreeable or inappropriate. Acknowledging such a possibility beforehand and considering your options for action will prepare you to resolve—or at least forestall—unpleasantness before it escalates into open conflict. Whether you are dealing with a member of the Board or an Association resident, you will be well served by having some guidelines for conflict resolution and a little psychological savvy.

If there is one absolute in any Community, it is that there will be at least one disruptive homeowner. You know who this person is. It is the person who is constantly badgering the manager or Board members about things that are wrong with the Community. It is the person who interrupts Board and Committee meetings with input and complaints that have either been dealt with before or have no bearing on the discussion at hand. It is the person who seems to be the bane of everybody's existence within the Community. The real question is, why does that person do what he or she does, and what can you do about it?

In a Community setting, even though the Association is a business and you are all part owners, it is not the same as in an employment situation. If an organization has a problem employee, steps can be taken to terminate that person's employment. Eventually, after creating enough problems and being the subject of enough documentation, that person gets fired.

In a Community setting, it is not that easy. The person who is the problem is also your neighbor. He or she also lives in the Community and is a part of the Association. He or she has just as much power and input as you—whether he or she holds an elected position or not.

It is very rare that a resident creates such grave problems that steps need to be taken to remove the person from the Community. In most cases, the disruptive homeowner is just that—disruptive. As a result, you have to figure out how to address the disruptive behaviors and calm the homeowner to the greatest extent possible.

While you may not completely solve the problem, any decrease in the problems the homeowner creates will be a relief to you and to the Community.

## Disruptive Behaviors

Fortunately, the number of disruptive homeowners in a Community is usually small, so they are easy to spot. It does not matter what they are dissatisfied about—they are simply dissatisfied and very vocal about it.

Disruptive behaviors range from displays of noisy grandstanding and filibustering at meetings, to letter-writing campaigns against other residents, Board or Committee members, or management. At Board meetings, disruptive homeowners will take up inordinate amounts of time belaboring unimportant details or decisions already made. They will interrupt—loudly—when others are speaking, and then complain that they are not being given a fair hearing.

Sometimes these homeowners will misuse resident lists to pursue letter-writing campaigns against those they think are treating them unfairly. Such letter-writing campaigns may follow a Board or other meeting, during which the dissatisfied homeowner did not fulfill his or her purpose and left the meeting still dissatisfied.

If an election is in the foreseeable future, these letter-writing campaigns may increase. Disruptive homeowners do not necessarily want to serve on Boards or Committees themselves, but they may want to make sure that their cronies get elected. The easiest way to make that happen, from their perspective, is to pursue a negative campaign against those who have not let them have their way.

Disruptive homeowners will make sure that their voices are heard—whether or not what they have to say has value or anyone wants to hear their message. The sad thing is, by the time they have established themselves as disruptive, even when they do have input of significance, no one wants to listen anymore.

## Reasons for being Disruptive

Problem owners may exhibit disruptive behavior that is willful, negative, petulant, aggressive, subversive, or even violent. Whether it results from poor communication, lack of insight, or psychological disorder, such behavior must be taken seriously and handled with respect. Equally, the needs of the disruptive individual must be managed so that they do not derail the ongoing functions of the Association.

Disruptive homeowners are disruptive when they have or can create an audience—and that is the first clue to why they act as they do. In some cases, disruptive homeowners do not have an agenda or purpose to their disruptions. They just want attention. In other cases, they are pursuing a clear agenda.

Toxic behavior may in fact have nothing to do with Association matters. The individual may be negative, angry, frustrated, bereaved, or even in physical pain, and may lack the skills or insight to manage such personal matters, allowing him or her to poison his or her interactions within the Association.

The individual may be seeking personal power to compensate for feelings of ineffectiveness. The person may fear the loss of his or her property—both physical and financial—through mismanagement. A lone voice of dissent may seem disruptive to a powerful majority, but it may actually be struggling to represent the valid rights of a minority. On the other hand, the resident may simply have too much time on his or her hands.

Perhaps the disruptive individual wants to force a neighbor to move because he or she does not like the neighbor. Maybe he or she owns multiple units in the Community and is trying to buy up more, and cannot do so unless some people move out. Some people simply have control complexes or were never taught polite behaviors.

Disruptive homeowners sometimes act the way they do because they are expressing their fears in the only way they know how. They might not understand how to present an argument or issue for consideration. They might believe that the Board, Committees, or management have missed crucial information that could have a direct impact on the Community, their investments, and their homes. They are simply afraid, and that leads them to behave in ways that are unacceptable in the forum they have chosen to air their fears.

No matter what the reason, disruptive homeowners disrupt because they want to draw attention to themselves and their issues. They believe they are right—no matter what. They believe that others are wrong, uninformed, or misinformed. Only they—that lone voice in the wilderness—have the right answer. To make sure that voice is heard, a disruptive homeowner also makes sure it is very loud.

The challenge for those on the Board, Committees, or in management is to determine, before taking action, why the homeowner is acting in the disruptive fashion. Board, Committee, and management members do not want to create future problems by overreacting to the disruptions. They must be calm, collected, and cognizant of why this disruptive person is behaving in such a difficult manner. Then, they can decide the appropriate course to take, both to address the homeowner's concerns and to reduce the disruptions.

## Handling Disruptive Situations

No matter what the circumstances, when someone becomes disruptive, you must not follow suit. Instead, show your respect for that person by listening attentively, communicating a clear response, considering alternatives, and seeking some form of compromise or consensus. In effect, you treat this person the way you would want to be treated if it were you bringing an issue to everyone's attention.

Listen—attentively and reserving judgment—to each speaker. Some disruptive individuals simply need to be heard. Lack of attention to the speaker, or worse, side conversations, undermine the potentially substantial benefit of such a forum. Resist responding in a manner that is defensive, accusatory, patronizing, sarcastic, withdrawn, or contemptuous—even if these actions are closer to your actual feelings. Such behavior may fuel hostilities and will certainly impede resolution.

Acknowledge the speaker's statements, even if you fervently disagree. Restating the problem in your own words is one way of doing this without compromising your position. Preserve respect between the parties. Remember that you will still be neighbors once this storm has passed. Be prepared to cite Association policies that govern the matters being discussed and limit the Association's ability to make immediate changes.

It is important that you show respect to these homeowners for a number of reasons. First, you have to protect your own integrity. Your behaviors are a reflection of the person you are—generous, respectful, attentive. You want to demonstrate those aspects of yourself both as a means of lessening conflict and modeling more appropriate behaviors.

Also, if the problem escalates—which sometimes happens—you do not want to put yourself into a position where you can be considered liable or culpable for any bad behaviors you may have demonstrated. Stay calm, cool, and in control.

Surprisingly, if the disruption occurs in a meeting, you are in the best position to keep that control. Meetings are structured events. Specific time is given for discussion of each issue. Even the open discussion times are limited so that each person can have his or her say, but the time to do so is restricted by the agenda.

Given that you have probably identified this person and the issue he or she wants to discuss, allow him or her the opportunity to do so, but begin by setting the time limit for his or her comments. For the sake of fairness, you should probably begin any person's speaking time by stating the time available for the discussion or his or her comments.

If the disruptive person is not a member of the Board or Committee that is meeting, and his or her comments are coming from the audience, open the question time with the statement that each questioner will have a certain number of minutes for his or her comments. Then, keep to the schedule.

If the disrupter is on the Board or Committee that is meeting, begin each topic area with the reminder that a specific number of minutes has been set for this discussion. You may also want to say that you want to get as much input as possible from all members. That will allow you to cut off the disruptive discussion, should it occur.

If the comments are being made as asides and not part of the discussion, stop those behaviors right away. Private conversation is never acceptable during a meeting. Do not ask them what they have been saying or to tell everyone their thoughts. Simply stop their conversation as soon as it begins. (Try saying, "Excuse me, can we please have one speaker at a time? I believe Ms. X has the floor.") Do not wait for it to become intrusive to the meeting. It must be stopped as soon as it begins.

It does not matter if you are the Board or Committee chair. Either you ask that the behavior stops or move that the chair put a stop to the conversation. It is disruptive and keeps the business at hand from being completed.

Sometimes the disruptions occur because of antipathy or dislike between two people. If that is the case and the matter is personal, ask them to resolve it privately. If the issue concerns the Association, then either it should be scheduled for discussion at the appropriate meeting or a neutral third party should mediate the disagreement.

Be aware that disagreements can, if not addressed appropriately, escalate into legal matters that must be addressed by the Association's legal representative. In all cases, due process must be followed to protect the Association from future liability or other problems. If a matter seems to have the potential to escalate toward legal liability, make sure you inform your legal counsel early and get their input as to the actions that should be taken.

**EXAMPLE:** One Association had a disruptive homeowner who started a letter-writing campaign against one of its Board members. Allegations and accusations without foundation were being made and broadcast through these letters to others throughout the Community. The Board member had to make a decision. Should he treat these letters as just the ravings of a dissatisfied homeowner, or were there potentially larger implications that needed to be addressed?

The Board member chose to inform the Association's legal counsel of the letters and provide copies that he had been able to get from some of his friends in the Community. Because the accusations were about the business of the Association and potential misdeeds by this Board member, the legal counsel did become involved.

First, it was important to determine that none of the allegations were true. From there, the issues of libel and slander needed to be brought to the complaining homeowner's attention. That homeowner was, in fact, putting his own legal welfare at risk because of his letter-writing campaign.

Ultimately, the homeowner provided a written apology to the Board member and a letter to all residents certifying that the accusations made had no basis in fact. Eventually the homeowner moved away, but even before that occurred, a potentially explosive legal situation was avoided.

The disruptive behavior may occur outside of the meeting environment, disrupting your peace of mind. While private conversation is productive for building relationships within the Association, it is not the best forum for airing grievances. When cornered by a problem owner, suggest that the matter be taken up—in a timely manner—before a Committee of other owners or the Board of Directors.

The main thing to be aware of in dealing with disruptive homeowners is that they are, intentionally or not, sabotaging the success of the Community and the Association. Their concerns may be well-founded, but their way of dealing with them may create great problems within the Community.

Make sure that the rules of the Community and the Association are being followed and be vigilant in taking appropriate action. The goal in dealing with a disruptive homeowner is to allay his or her concerns and move forward. The process of doing so is invariably more complicated than its outcome, so be patient but be tough. You can create a successful solution for all involved by understanding the reasons for the disruptions and then acting appropriately.

## THE THREE Ps

When residents are asked to name the three biggest problems they face in their Community Association, the *Three Ps* usually appear very close to the top of the list: people, pets, and parking. Conflicts exist in neighborhoods everywhere, but because of the proximity and ownership issues involved with Association living, they are intensified and sometimes very difficult to ignore. It should not be too surprising that everyone does not always get along with their neighbors all the time.

## Dealing with Difficult People

Neighbors have probably been feuding since long before the Hatfields and McCoys faced off across the banks of Tug Fork, and it is unlikely you will be able to resolve those issues once and for all. However, there are some recurring themes in association *people problems*, and awareness can contribute to an easing of tensions.

When asked to describe the qualities (beyond "I just do not like them") that are most irksome in their neighbors and most likely to lead to conflict, Community Association members say that their difficult neighbors are:

- power grabbers;
- control freaks;
- messy;
- always late;
- rude and inconsiderate (including not listening);
- irresponsible and unreliable;
- unfair;
- rule-breakers;
- noisy;
- critical;
- blamers;
- nosy;
- disruptive;
- snobs;
- unfriendly; and,
- unsympathetic.

Fortunately, very few (if any) of your neighbors are sociopaths. They are mostly ordinary people, living the best life they know how.

Along with behavioral concerns, there are also profound personal issues that can aggravate day-to-day interactions, such as:

- political differences, including differences over environmental issues that may, directly or indirectly, affect the Association's property;
- economic differences and different economic priorities;
- cultural differences; and,
- physical and emotional boundary issues.

With so much potential for conflict, it is a wonder that so many Associations manage to maintain the peace and operate as smoothly as they do. To minimize interpersonal problems, the following are some suggestions for Board members and managers.

- Get a suggestion box and encourage residents to use it—anonymously, if they want. Take suggestions seriously and post them, along with answers, on a bulletin board.

- Invite homeowners to sit on Committees, even if they are not Board members. Allowing people to voice their opinions and participate in decisions strengthens their feeling of ownership.

- Find roles of responsibility for individuals who seem to do nothing but complain. Even a very small task—arranging flowers for the lobby, maintaining the bulletin board, spearheading a healthy lifestyles Committee—can satisfy such a person's need for recognition and power.

- If your Board meetings are closed to Association members, consider opening them.

- Try something creative with your Association meeting agenda occasionally, such as letting a non-Board member or someone other than the President lead the meeting.

- Avoid making unrealistic promises (repairs, improvements, etc.) and inform residents immediately if there is any change to scheduled or promised work.

- Encourage residents to report problems as soon as they notice them. Small problems are easier and less expensive to repair, and less likely to inspire anger.

- Respect residents' privacy. If a face-to-face meeting is required to deal with a critical issue, call or leave a note in advance to schedule the meeting. Dropping in at their homes unannounced or cornering people at the pool or in the elevator is almost always inappropriate.

- Spend a moment to do a mental role reversal when dealing with others. Picture yourself in their situation, and imagine how you would feel and act.

- Consider adding a volunteer ombudsman to your Association personnel. This could be someone trained in psychology, conflict resolution, or mediation, who can help residents find common ground when they are in conflict.

♦ Encourage occasional Association-wide activities—and let residents do the planning. A barbecue, garage sale, or pancake brunch encourages camaraderie.

♦ Let residents plant and maintain a vegetable garden—even if it is tiny or has to be planted in pots.

♦ Encourage residents to participate in Association book groups, bridge clubs, walking or jogging groups, or other small group activities.

♦ Offer educational activities with invited speakers, such as how-to classes, lectures on local history, or book reviews—and put a homeowner in charge.

♦ Take time, regularly and often, to talk with neighbors individually. Listen to what they have to say.

♦ Be friendly, but not pushy. Make eye contact, smile, and say hello to your neighbors when you see them.

♦ Use the Association's bulletin board, newsletter, or website to acknowledge positive people and accomplishments.

♦ Do not contribute to the gossip and rumor mill, and be especially cautious about turning Board meetings into gossip sessions. Proximity breeds gossip. While it can be a fairly harmless way for people to blow off steam, it can also lead to divisive factions and reduced trust. If you are able to defuse a rumor, do so immediately and publicly.

♦ Consider that *you* may be part of the problem—that something in your personality or your personal agenda may cause other people to see you as a difficult person.

♦ Acknowledge that, no matter what you do, some people simply do not want to participate. Some people will always find matters, large or small, to complain about, and some people are probably unsuited for Community living—but you are stuck with them and need to make the best of it.

Community Association living puts people in close proximity with others who are strangers—people with whom you may have few shared values. Such closeness, compounded by the stress of everyday living, may lower your reserves of tolerance, shorten tempers, and make people forget the courtesies that lubricate human relations. As Board members and managers, you can use your leadership role to set a high standard by exercising exceptional courtesy, restraint, compassion, and good humor in your interactions with your neighbors. By dealing thoughtfully and respectfully with difficult people, and acting as positive role models for your neighbors, you can help people see and appreciate the many benefits of Community Association living.

## Taking the Bite Out of Pet Management

Few things have the potential for excesses of both romance and rancor as the subject of pets. Where a closed door, a fence, or a leash could at one time resolve most problems related to animal companions, today more and more people find themselves in court, defending a beloved pet against mistreatment by another animal, a person, a local ordinance—or a Community Association.

Nearly 60% of American households have dogs, cats, or both, and those numbers are increasing. Also on the rise are exotic pets, from armadillos to wombats and everything in between.

Most pet owners treat their animals as members of the family and bristle at the suggestion that they, and their pets, must abide by special rules. It is the development of such rules that confronts every Community Association—a matter that must be handled with wisdom, logic, and knowledgeable professional help.

While there is little doubt that animals bring great pleasure—and even improved health—to their owners, that benefit is not necessarily shared by the neighbors. Some of the recurring problems that put animals and their owners into conflict with their neighbors include:

- aggression toward people or other animals, which can include biting, teeth-baring, growling, scratching, lunging, and other displays of aggressive behavior;
- noise;
- animal waste;
- number of animals;

- odors;
- property damage, including chewing, scratching, digging, climbing, or destruction of personal or common area property, furniture, carpets, flower beds, or other landscaping;
- where animals are allowed;
- who controls the animal, including animal escapes;
- obedience and manners, including unwelcome jumping;
- health concerns, including allergies and pet-to-pet contagion; and,
- environmental concerns, such as pet dishes that could attract wild animals.

The Community Association's challenge is to create a workable set of rules that will satisfy both those who share their homes with animals and those who do not. The rules need to define terms carefully and explain policies and penalties clearly. (For example, a rule prohibiting dogs and cats might easily be interpreted to allow ferrets and monkeys. A rule that excludes all but service animals might be questioned if a pet is prescribed by a doctor for the owner's emotional comfort, but is not actually certified as a service animal.)

Unfortunately, there is no perfect time to introduce rules regarding pets. Even a brand-new association will encounter problems with buyers who have treasured pets. Rules that seem suitable when a Community Association is first established might prove to be unworkable once the full complement of residents is in place.

However, the rules must get written or amended. Some points to consider when taking on the task include the following.

- Many jurisdictions are involved in the regulation of animals— even on private property. The federal *Fair Housing Act*, as well as the state and local municipalities, may affect the Association's ability to create binding rules. This will vary from location to location. Find out which rulings are in force in your area. The Humane Society may also be able to provide some guidance.
- If you are adding or changing pet policies, examine the current Homeowners Association documents for all references to pets and an understanding of exactly what is required to amend the rules.

- Review the Association's insurance policy and keep handy any references to animals. (Individual homeowner policies exclude a growing number of dog breeds.)
- Consult with the Humane Society or the U.S. Department of Agriculture to establish a list of currently unacceptable exotic or wild animals that are occasionally (and unwisely) kept as pets.
- Consider establishing a Pet Legal Committee that includes pet owners and nonowners, and both Board members and non-Board members. This group would be charged with researching, developing, presenting, and enforcing the pet rules, under the appropriate blessing of the full Board. Involving Community members in this controversial matter is likely to result in more cooperation when the rules are introduced and enforced.
- Consider taking a pet census to get a better idea of what you are dealing with. Survey both numbers and breeds of animals.
- Draft policies that are useful, reasonable, clear, and logical. Look for loopholes and try to clarify any terms that can have multiple interpretations.
- Have the drafted rules reviewed by an attorney with expertise in fair housing law.
- Once the Board has approved the rules, follow the Association's CC&Rs to provide adequate notice to the Community and arrange for a vote, if necessary.
- Provide a printed copy of the new or revised rules to all residents and nonresident owners. Distribute copies of the rules each year at the annual meeting.
- Post signage as appropriate (for example, "No Animals in the Pool").
- Enforce rules promptly, compassionately, and even-handedly.
- Implement an educational program to complement the pet rules. Consider adding a "pet corner" to the Association's newsletter, website, or bulletin board with updates, reminders, and other useful information (names of local dog walkers, upcoming vaccination or spay/neuter clinics, obedience classes, and so on). Invite a veterinarian or someone from animal control or the Humane Society to address homeowners at an Association meeting.

- Make sure that new residents are aware of pet rules before they move in. Take the time to explain the rules and answer questions for new residents, and consider requiring a "read and understood" signature on a copy of the rules.

Some additional things to address in your rules concerning pets include the following.

- Overall policy, such as no pets or pets restricted by size, weight, breed, or species. Even a *pets welcome* policy must be defined clearly.
- Policy regarding service animals. This is a very complex area. Consult an attorney knowledgeable about the Fair Housing Act and the most recent court rulings on this subject. Specify what registration, certification, and documentation is required for an animal to qualify.
- Grandfathered animals. The rules may allow current pet owners to keep their animals, but they should be very specific about what happens when the animal gives birth or dies, when the owner (or the pet) moves to another unit, or when the owner dies.
- Policy for fees and deposits required for pet owners, as well as any special insurance, inspections, vaccination certificates, etc. Establish a filing system to make sure that this material is kept current.
- Where pets are allowed. Is there a designated pet run and who is responsible for cleanup? Include policy regarding leashes, muzzles, obedience training, and voice commands, as appropriate.
- Waste management, including information about location of trash bins, availability of pooper scoopers, dumping of cat boxes, accidents in common areas, etc.
- Cleanliness of common areas, including provisions for wet or muddy animals during inclement weather and policies regarding pets in pools, fountains, and other landscaping features.
- To whom the rules apply (i.e., the pet owner or the owner's family, pet sitters, or anyone who might be caring for the pet at the time). Make sure the policy covers renters, guests, and visitors to the Community.

- How the Association will handle (or not handle) pet owner versus pet owner or pet versus pet problems.
- Responsibility for observing and obeying posted signage.
- Policy regarding non-pet animal interactions—bird feeders, feeding stray animals, placing pet dishes outdoors, etc.
- Waiver process for requesting and dealing with exceptions to the pet rules.
- System for submitting complaints.
- Method of investigating complaints.
- Steps to be taken in enforcement.
- Penalties for failure to comply with rules.

In spite of your best efforts to create well-reasoned rules, there will be Association members who feel that the rules do not apply to them or their pets. Unfortunately, a powerful Board member could be one of them, and the association must be prepared to deal with this eventuality.

Some residents may feel that their pets do not count, or that their little gecko, garter snake, or gerbil is so small and quiet that no one will ever know. Residents will be quick to make excuses for their lapses. For example, "The UPS driver left the gate open"; "I had a migraine and could not take Fluffy outside myself so I just opened the door"; "That wasn't a bite, it was just a puppy kiss"; or, "Oh no, my Fifi would never do that!"

You may also find that there are chronic complainers—residents who are afraid of, allergic to, or not fond of animals. These complainers may also be using this issue as a way to get attention.

Nonetheless, every waiver request, complaint, and infraction must be handled promptly and seriously, regardless of who is making the complaint and whose pet is involved. Over time, as Association members see that the rules are being implemented even-handedly, they will be more willing to comply.

## Community Traffic and Parking Management
While probably not as contentious as pet rules, the development and enforcement of vehicle rules can be a thorn in the side of any

Community Association. Straightforward standards developed when the Community was built—resident parking, guest parking, fire lanes, loading zones, and so on—can devolve into annoying or even dangerous problems for the Board, management, and residents.

The most common vehicle-related problems include:

- resident cars parked in guest parking spots;
- cars parked in loading zones or fire lanes;
- vehicles blocking driveways, ramps, elevators, fire exits, or stair-wells, or otherwise impeding ingress and egress;
- non-permitted cars parked in posted handicap parking spaces;
- idling vehicles left unattended;
- noisy revving of cars or motorcycles or excessively amplified music in cars;
- residents exceeding the allowed number of cars per unit;
- using parking spaces for storage of personal items;
- using parking spaces or other Association space for car washing or auto repairs;
- vehicles leaking oil onto the garage floor; and,
- exceeding the posted speed limit on Association property.

As with pet policies, vehicle rules must be reasonable, clear, and enforced consistently. There should be an established protocol for making and handling complaints, and defined penalties for infractions. On page 119 is a sample list of rules that has worked well for one Association.

Residents are more likely to comply with rules if parking areas are well-maintained. Management should see that parking areas are swept, light bulbs are in working order, doors and gates are operating properly, and floors are periodically steam cleaned to remove stains. To encourage the use of bicycles and to keep them out of the parking area, the Association may want to designate an adjacent covered area as a bicycle parking zone and to install racks where bikes can be locked up safely.

Community Associations may also be faced with other challenges to established parking policies. For example, a new owner may require a handicap parking space large enough to accommodate a lift van, but his or her assigned space is too small. In making reasonable accommodations, the Board may be required to reassign parking spaces, which may require the rewriting of the CC&Rs.

Parking rules should be reviewed by the Board periodically, posted on a bulletin board in the garage, and distributed to residents each year at the annual meeting.

In order to protect the rights, safety, and comfort of all Association residents, the Board of Directors and Management have established the following rules, which apply to all owners and their family members, guests, subtenants, employees, and other visitors.

1. Parking spaces are approved for vehicle parking only. No personal items of any sort, including bicycles, may be left or stored in parking spaces.
2. Vehicles must not exceed 10 miles per hour on Association property.
3. Residents may park only in their assigned spaces.
4. Only vehicles displaying handicap parking permits may use designated handicap parking spaces. Vehicles in violation are subject to immediate towing.
5. Parked vehicles must not block or restrict access to other parking spaces—even for a short time.
6. Idling vehicles must not be left unattended.
7. Residents are allowed a maximum of five guest parking spaces at one time unless previously authorized by Management. Guest parking permits must be displayed; they may be obtained from Lobby Security.
8. All vehicles on Association property must be maintained in running condition and kept reasonably clean. Vehicles must not leak fluids or emit fumes that could cause a health or environmental hazard. Management reserves the right to deny parking privileges to vehicles that are excessively dirty, rusted, or in serious disrepair.
9. Vehicles may not be washed or repaired on Association property.
10. The center of the parking plaza must be kept clear at all times for emergency vehicle access.
11. Campers and other oversize vehicles may not be parked in the parking area.
12. Vehicle and pedestrian doors to the garage must not be blocked open at any time.
13. Loss of garage door openers must be reported to management immediately.
14. While the Association is not responsible for damage to persons, vehicles, or other property, or loss of property from vehicles or garage, crimes should be reported immediately to police and management.
15. It is the responsibility of residents to inform their guests of parking restrictions and to ensure that the parking code is observed.
16. Vehicles in violation of this Association Parking Code are subject to ticketing and/or towing at the owner's expense, and homeowners may be subject to a fine.

# –7–
# PROACTIVE AND PREVENTIVE FINANCIAL MANAGEMENT

In a Community, it is easy to forget that the Association is a business in and of itself. For the most part, homeowners do not think about the Association unless they are active on the Board or Committees—or something goes wrong in their home and they do not think that management's response is adequate.

In fact, the business of the Community is an ongoing, day-to-day activity that requires careful oversight and monitoring. Even though the Association is not a for-profit business, the same successful business tenets and processes that are used in small and large organizations worldwide must also be applied to the Association's business. The key to that success is that management think and act both proactively and preventively to ensure that before things go wrong, they have already been addressed—or at least the systems for addressing those problems are already in place.

It has been said that 97% of what goes on in any business or organization is predictable. You may not like it, but you know it is going to happen. Whether it is the sending of your monthly assessment bill; periodic assessment increases due to greater financial needs, carpet wear and tear in the common areas, the need for plumbing, and other maintenance activities; disruptive homeowners who do not follow the rules; or, anything else—you may not like it, but you know it is going to happen.

Knowing in advance that these situations will occur, the Board and manager should be prepared to handle them easily. Unfortunately, most Community Associations manage reactively rather than proactively. Often, you will hear things, such as, "Who thought that the carpet would wear out?" "The air conditioning ducts are leaking through the ceilings into two floors' worth of units! We need emergency repairs," or "How was I supposed to know that the assessments were going to go up—even though this is the first time in years?" When these issues are not addressed proactively, they result in the need for special assessments and other measures that could and should have easily been avoided.

## KEEPING A FORWARD VIEW

The trick to successful management is to always look at the 97% that is predictable and plan for it. You may not know when things will go wrong, but rather than be surprised, you take preemptive measures to ensure that the impact will be as small as possible. In the best case scenarios, the planning is so good and thorough, and the follow-up action so well executed, that there really are no surprises. Everything consistently runs smoothly.

Why, then, do most Associations find themselves managing backwards—or reactively—rather than forwards and proactively? In most cases, the Board and management either do not think about or know how to manage in a forward-looking way. In other cases, it is because the task simply seems too daunting.

In fact, managing forward is much easier, less expensive, less time-consuming, and much less anxiety-producing than managing reactively. You simply need to know what to manage, take on those aspects that make sense for the Board or Committees, and ensure that you have the right team surrounding your Association to provide support in all those areas that require special expertise.

By managing proactively, you and your Association are practicing the best form of risk management. You are looking at the contingencies of what might occur, preparing for them, and taking ongoing action on those items and issues that require day-to-day oversight. There is no better way to reduce the risk to your Association than by taking a proactive and preventive stance.

# TAKING A TEAM APPROACH

Real success in forward planning comes with the establishment of a team to surround you and your Association. This team consists of all the experts you must have available to you for the specific knowledge and guidance that they bring.

In addition, because financial matters are so comprehensive, the Board, Committees, management, volunteers, employees, outside contractors, and others who can contribute vital information to the process should be prepared to participate in working with your experts. This will ensure that the financial picture provided to the Association and its homeowners is as complete as possible.

In an earlier chapter, the importance of finding the appropriate attorney for your Association was discussed. As you will see, in the arena of finance, it is just as crucial that you have a financial expert available to your Association, and to work with your Board and management. As was mentioned, the Association is best advised to use outside contractors to avoid any appearance of impropriety or actual conflict of interest. Be just as proactive in ensuring that you have the most objective experts as you are in ensuring that they have the expertise that you and your Association require.

# BASIC CONSIDERATIONS IN FINANCIAL MANAGEMENT

If the governing documents, CC&Rs, Bylaws, and House Rules are the skeleton of the Association, then financial management is its lifeblood. No matter what other steps are taken, the only way to ensure the ongoing viability of the Community is to carefully and thoughtfully manage the Association's financial affairs.

Realistically, the Board members and management cannot do this on their own. There are specific skills required to fully understand and manage the current and future fiscal requirements of the Association. As such, if your Association does not already have a certified public accountant (CPA) on retainer, make that one of your first action items.

In choosing a CPA, be aware that there are different areas of specialization in accounting. You want a CPA who specializes in

Community Association finance. If you do not know where you can find one, ask Board members or managers of other local Community Associations. You can also contact the *Community Associations Institute* (CAI), a nationwide organization dedicated to Community Association managers and homeowners, to find out who they might have in their database in your area. Look at ads in the local Community Association organization magazine, or attend meetings of the CAI or your local organization.

Do your research, get references, and always be aware that this person will be working closely with the finances of the Association. You want someone you can trust.

In the meantime, the four particular areas about which the Board members and homeowners must be knowledgeable are:

1. operating budgets;
2. reserves;
3. investments; and,
4. financial oversight.

Homeowners and Board members must be prepared to participate in the financial health and well-being of the Association. To that end, some basic knowledge is required.

Be aware that this chapter does not propose or intend to be comprehensive in the area of finance. It is designed to give you the guidance and information you and your Association need to know what steps you should take next and how you might proceed.

## OPERATING BUDGETS

For many Associations, the budget is something the Board does about two weeks before the annual meeting. They think about all the regular and not so regular expenses the Association must cover—cleaning crew, trash collection, insurance, taxes—and then they wonder what they left out and hope that the assessments will cover everything. In such cases, the Board members mistake the budget as a task instead of understanding it as the basis of the Association's financial strategy—not just for this year, but preferably, for as many as five years to come.

Putting together an operating budget is tedious, but it is not as difficult as it seems. The easiest way to get the right budget for the strategy of the Association is to follow some simple steps—in the order that they appear in the following pages.

## Step One: Setting a Financial Strategy

The Board members should begin the budgeting process by having a session dedicated to discussing the strategy for the Community. Is your Community in a transitional area that will require upgrades to your property? Does the property simply need a face-lift to make any cosmetic improvements inside and out that have been lacking in years past?

How well have the operating systems of the property been maintained? What steps need to be taken to ensure the operating safety of the property—whether the computer equipment used by the management office or the HVAC systems?

Include discussion about repairs that have potential liability for the Association. Are your sidewalks and walkways in the common areas smooth and safe? Are weeds growing through the paving? Are the garage entrances, exits, and parking areas well maintained? How long has it been since the roof was repaired or replaced? Are the grounds appealing and well maintained? If there is a pool, Jacuzzi, gym, tennis court, barbecue, or other common entertainment area, is it well maintained? Is the equipment safe?

All of these and more have implications for the financial strategy and operating budget for the Association. Granted, it may not be possible to do everything at once. However, at least by identifying these and other necessary expenditures, the Association can start prioritizing its expenses and begin the budgeting process.

## Step Two: Analyze the Association's Past Years' Records

Gather together all the financial records for the Association—the most recent reserve study, expense records, tax and revenue information—anything you can get your hands on. If at all possible, have the past five years' records available so that you can recognize and prepare for trends.

There may be changes in utility or insurance costs that might have an impact on the Association. The payroll of the Association may have to grow or you might need to be prepared for additional expenses for expert assistance. If the economy is in the process of an upturn or a downturn, that should also be taken into consideration, as it could have an impact on the revenues for the Association.

Make sure you look carefully at the projections for and timing of major repairs and replacements cited in the reserve study. These must be factored into your budget. As a result of your strategic planning session, you may find that a more recent reserve study is required, if the one you have is outdated or no longer altogether applicable.

### Step Three: Estimate Costs Based on the Strategic Plan

Once you know your strategy and financial history, the next step is to prioritize the additional expenses for which you should be prepared and estimate how much each will cost.

Some of your expenses are regular and consistent. These include insurance premiums for the year or the salary for the manager. Other expenses are regular but not consistent. These include legal or accounting fees, printing and postage expenses, maintenance costs, and others. In these cases, you should establish an estimated budget range and plan accordingly.

Remember that not everything has to be paid for all at once, and not all of the Association's monies will or should be spent at the beginning of the year. Spread out improvements to balance with the costs of maintenance, repairs, and the growth of the reserves.

### Step Four: Establish and Monitor the Budget

Finally, taking all the information at hand, establish a budget that is workable and reasonable for the Community. Do not budget down to the last penny. Leave some money for contingencies for which you could not have been prepared.

Do not allow personal preferences or agendas to come into the budgeting process. Just because a Board member wants to create a slush fund against possible future and as yet unidentified expenditures, does not mean that assessments should be increased. Each expense is traceable and trackable—and the Board is accountable to the homeowners for its fiscal thoughtfulness and thoroughness.

To that end, monitoring systems should be established that are part of the monthly Board meetings and information to homeowners. A simple, one-page form showing revenues, monthly expenditures (including for what) with year-to-date totals, reserve account balances and expenditures, and so on should be provided to all Board members and meeting attendees. Copies should also be available in the management office at all times for homeowners to review. There should be no secrets in the budget.

Finally, give yourselves enough time to complete this process. The first time you go through it, you may decide to take four to six months to ensure that you have all the information necessary. In future years it will be quicker, but you should still allow yourselves four months before the annual meeting to complete the process.

## RESERVES

The purpose of the Association's financial reserves is to ensure that the Community has the money it needs for necessary repairs and replacements. The reserves represent the preventive and proactive financial thinking of the Association.

There are two types of reserve accounts that should be kept by the Association. The first is the one with which most Associations are familiar. These reserves are the ones already earmarked by the Association for future repairs based on the Association's regularly scheduled reserve study. The second type of reserves is a contingency reserve recommended by the *Federal Housing Authority* (FHA), which is a governmental agency that makes recommendations and policy in all areas of housing—including Community Associations. Contingency reserves are not as commonly known or acted upon as the basic reserves. The contingency reserve should equal 3%–5% of the operating budget and be used exclusively for emergencies that might otherwise require a special assessment.

The combination of these two reserve accounts ensures that the Association and all the homeowners are as protected against the future as the Board can foresee. In fact, by having the two sets of reserves, each specifically used for its own purpose, the Association has not only accounted for the 97% of what happens that is predictable, but also for the 3% that is not.

While it is easy to establish the amount to be deposited into the contingency reserve once your budget is set, determining the basic reserve account monies requires a greater level of analysis and expertise. A full reserve study should be scheduled for at least every three years. This study—completed by experts in this field—allows the Board to determine what monies it will need to allocate and when.

Each year, during the budgeting process, the reserve study should be reviewed and updated. It may be that certain unexpected repairs have occurred that necessitated taking money from the contingency reserve. In such cases, the Board should determine whether this was an oversight in the reserve study and should have been expected.

If that is the case, the expense should become an expected repair or replacement, and in the future, be accounted for in the basic reserve account. If it is not the case, and the expense really was a one-off and should not be expected to recur, then it should be treated as the contingency it was.

Reserves are a planned expense for the Association. Reserve monies come from regular deposits of percentages of monthly assessments, commercial property rents, and if well invested, from interest earned by the existing reserves. As such, in developing the budget, the Board must carefully analyze the reserve study before determining whether increased assessments might be required for reserve related expenses.

Finally, reserve monies should be held wholly separate and apart from the operating budget. Just as with the budget, there must be a reserve account planning and use, so that Board members, management, and homeowners can see exactly how much money is in reserve; in what types of investments; how much is scheduled for use; and, how much has already been used.

Reserves are the life savings of the Association—always planning for the future and ensuring that the Community will provide safe and comfortable housing for the owners.

# INVESTMENTS

To be fiscally prudent, the Association needs an investment strategy that is in keeping with its overall strategy and designed to ensure the long-term safety of the Community. In order to develop such a strategy, it is necessary to work with a qualified investment advisor who has background in assisting Community Associations.

There are a variety of fee structures offered by investment advisors. The Association will be best protected if it selects an advisor who is paid a flat annual fee for services. That way, the Association is better assured that the advisor is not building extra fees by churning the business from investment to investment with a fee being paid at each move. The advisor should have no other agenda for the Association than to provide prudent financial guidance and advice.

There are three primary considerations in establishing the Association's investment strategy. It is important that these considerations be addressed in this order to protect the Association and its funds.

- ◆ The first consideration is that the money is safely deposited in low-risk investments and held in insured institutions. Your investment advisor will help you determine how best to achieve this goal.
- ◆ The second concern is that the money be available when needed, which means that the reserve study should be carefully analyzed to determine how much money will be needed and when. That way, money will be liquid and available when you need it, at no penalty to the Association.
- ◆ The third and final consideration is the yield or return on investment. Board members should exercise caution and restraint, and well-thought fiscal prudence, to protect the monies already in hand while growing them carefully for the future.

It is easy in these days of online trading to want to make a quick buck. That is the last thing you want done with the investment monies. The money belongs to the Association—not to the Board members or to some friend of a Board member who is a financial whiz and made a killing trading online.

Always remember that the funds that are being invested are the lifeblood of the Association. The keys to a successful investment strategy for the Association are being conservative and keeping the money at minimum risk.

## FINANCIAL OVERSIGHT

There are a number of tasks that must be regularly completed to ensure that the financial needs of the Community are being well-managed. Some of these are completed by your CPA, others by your investment advisor, your bookkeeper, Finance Committee members, and so on. The important thing is to know that they are necessary and make sure they are addressed.

Each year, a financial analysis should be completed for the Board and homeowners. This should be completed by your CPA with the full cooperation of the Board, Committees, management, employees, vendors, outside contractors, and others with information to be provided.

The analysis results in a management letter generated by the CPA, detailing the findings on financial systems, taxes, reserves, documents, and internal controls. Recommendations should be provided to the Board by the CPA, and the management letter provided to the homeowners at the annual meeting. During the year, the Board should receive monthly financial statements from the CPA with a quarterly reconciliation of all accounts and investments.

Policies must be developed and enforced by the Board regarding the Association's investment policy, control of reserves, signatory control, collections, kickback protection and prohibition, and maintenance of separate accounts for the operating budget and reserve monies. All of these policies create a check-and-balance system necessary to keep the Association safe and secure.

In addition, Directors and Officers (D&O) insurance should be provided for the Board members. The manager and employees, as well as any volunteers who handle Association funds, should be adequately bonded to secure the Association's funds.

Work with your attorney and CPA to make sure that all policies and procedures necessary to protect the Association are in place. Take the time to make sure that your documents are up to date and available at all times, in case they are needed. By taking a preventive, proactive stance regarding your Association's finances, you will ensure that you can feel safe and secure in your own home and Community.

# —8—
# PLANNING AND MONITORING

The best-run organizations operate by the adage, *plan the work and work the plan*. While it may seem overly simplistic, the challenges associated with planning and execution are many. Further, the key to success is having monitoring systems in place so that progress—or the lack thereof—in completing the plan is obvious.

Planning is far too often overlooked or glossed over by Community Associations. They operate in a reactive mode, taking care of problems as they occur, finding themselves mired in legal and financial troubles, and always running to keep up. This is neither good business nor necessary.

Why, then, are planning and monitoring so rarely addressed and completed as they should be? Mostly, because both are time-consuming and there is a comforting, though erroneous, belief that someday it will no longer be necessary to run just to stay in place. That day will never come unless something is done to change the way the Association operates.

For homeowners, the planning and monitoring systems are crucial. Whether you are a homeowner who only attends the annual meeting and is never seen throughout the year, or a volunteer homeowner who actively participates on Committees or the Board of Directors, you must be able to see where the Community stands at any given time.

In the previous chapter, this was discussed in relation to finance. That same understanding is crucial when it comes to the present and future-oriented operational planning that the Community must do to protect itself.

Monitoring forms are visual indicators of the progress and status of the Community and its Association. Whether looking to see if certain cosmetic projects are scheduled for your common areas, or checking on the preventive maintenance activities for the plumbing and heating systems before an expected cold winter, each homeowner must have access to up-to-date information whenever it is requested.

As such, it is in the best interests of the Board and management to develop the planning and monitoring systems that will be maintained throughout the year—and to use them regularly and consistently. Frankly, if either the Board or management is not doing so, they are not doing their jobs.

## PRIORITY AREAS

There are four priority areas in planning and monitoring:
1. preventive maintenance systems;
2. emergency preparedness systems;
3. preferred supplier systems; and,
4. association operations.

While each is addressed separately, it is crucial that the Association take appropriate action to ensure that planning, execution, and monitoring for each priority area is ongoing. Only by doing so can homeowners be assured that their Community is truly prepared and protected for the present and the future.

This chapter should not be treated as a comprehensive guide to all the planning and monitoring activities that should be undertaken. Remember the team that surrounds you. By accessing and utilizing the expertise of your legal counsel, accountant, vendors, consultants, Board, Committee members, and other volunteers, you can be assured that your planning process is as comprehensive and customized to the needs of your Community as possible.

## PREVENTIVE MAINTENANCE SYSTEMS

Think about this scenario. You see paint markings on a wall in a common area that are not supposed to be there and you think,

"The manager will take care of that. It is not a problem." For a while, it is all right with you.

Time goes on and somehow the markings are never fixed. Time passes, and every time you pass that spot those marks seem to get bigger. After enough time, they loom in your day-to-day life, eventually making you angry every time you walk by or even think about them. Even worse, because they were never addressed, other markings have grown up around them, and now the whole area looks a mess.

Welcome to a maintenance problem that is never addressed— and that is just a cosmetic example. You can be assured that if there are readily visible problems that are not being addressed, then there are a host of other problems within the common workings of the Community that are also being neglected. Preventive maintenance is too often treated as a luxury that no one really needs. This is absolutely wrong.

The key to long life and health of the Community—as well as to ensuring that your property value continues to grow—is the establishment of a preventive maintenance system that is implemented and monitored year in and year out.

The good news is that it is not difficult to design and maintain a preventive maintenance system for your Community. In fact, there are expert consultants who specialize in the design of such systems and can even provide preventive maintenance manuals for your Association to use.

This is an important consideration for the Association, as preventive maintenance plays an important part in your ability to determine your reserve requirements. By using an expert in the field, your Association is much more likely to get the depth and breadth of information it needs—as well as the resources to be able to address those needs in a timely manner.

As a starting point, the following are some of the steps you should take in developing your preventive maintenance plan. As you read through them, you will probably think that this is far too tedious a process. However, in the *plan the work and work the plan* world you are creating, once this process has been completed, maintenance can simply be scheduled and occur as necessary—leaving you without worries about safety, property values, or how well your Community is being maintained.

### Step One: Develop a Comprehensive Maintenance List

With your Association's management, take a walk through all the common areas of your Community. This is not a normal walk. This walk is the equivalent of a detailed tour of all the inner and outer workings of your Community.

Make a list of all the major systems and components that require maintenance. Do not worry how long the list is. In fact, the more comprehensive the list, the better prepared you will be in making your plan.

As you walk through your building, you know that the common areas need to be painted. So, painting goes on the list. When you list painting, you need to clarify that the building or buildings require interior and exterior painting. Your common areas may include elevators, solar energy systems, sidewalk paving, tennis courts, spa tub, plumbing and heating systems, gardens—whatever it is, write it down.

Further, keep in mind that just writing down "spa tub" or "pool" will not actually be enough. Eventually, you are going to have to look at grouting and tiling requirements for those facilities just as much as you look at the cleaning schedule and requirements. You cannot count on your pool cleaning service to report those types of problems to you.

Remember the sump pump in the garage or basement, intercom systems, security lights, sprinklers, overhead pipes in the garage, driveways, doorways (security and otherwise), carpets, windows, tree maintenance, and everything else.

Once you have completed the list as comprehensively as you can, look at vendor bills for the past three to five years to see if there is anything you left out. Include any detailed information on colors, components, vendors, and so on that will assist you in creating a complete and easy-to-implement list.

## Step Two: Prepare the List for a Maintenance Schedule

Taking the list you have generated, augment the information on the various components with as much information as you possibly can. Rather than just listing "exterior paint," identify the color and manufacturer of the paint. If you know when the building's exterior was last painted, include that information as well.

Equipment items on your list should include the manufacturer, where it is located, which parts and functions require regular service, who has provided that service in the past, and when any service was last performed. If you have service recommendations from the manufacturers or installers, include that information as part of this list.

For garden, paving, and other non-equipment items, the location, its service requirements, service provider, and when service was last performed should be included.

## Step Three: Develop the Maintenance Schedule

Taking all the information compiled, develop a preventive maintenance schedule for all the common areas, equipment, components, and the like that you have identified. Use the last serviced date as a starting point for your scheduling. If no such information is available, assess the risk of putting off maintenance and schedule accordingly.

Spread your maintenance plan out over the year. This will allow you to manage your costs better and to avoid traumatizing the Community with too much activity at one time.

Your costs will be affected by your scheduling. Be smart. Do not try to schedule weather-dependent activities in times when the weather is prohibitive (like roofing in the winter). This is a preventive system. You are trying to avoid emergency costs—do not build them into your plan if they can be avoided.

Review your reserve study to assess the expected lifetime of the various equipment and components. In some cases, general maintenance and small repairs will be adequate. However, when full repair and replacement is necessary as called for in your study, plan accordingly.

In addition, your maintenance vendors will be able to give you insight into when you might need to plan for repair or replacement of items that are not included in your reserve study. Make this process a collaborative one—working with your experts to ensure that the Association has developed a workable and dependable schedule for maintenance.

### Step Four: Manage the Plan

Just because you have compiled the list and have a schedule does not mean that it is going to be implemented. Ensure that at each month's Board meeting a copy of the preventive maintenance schedule is included in the materials for review. Check out how things are progressing and if the plan is being kept. Ask questions about maintenance items that were scheduled but did not occur.

Eventually, preventive maintenance will become so built into the system that you will be able to lessen your monitoring and oversight. Until that happens, however, keep an eye open.

## EMERGENCY PREPAREDNESS

Whether you live in earthquake, hurricane, tornado, or blizzard country, you and your Community should always be prepared for an emergency. Emergency preparedness has too often been dumped into the overall category of *risk management*, which is erroneously defined as making sure your Community and Association have adequate insurance. Risk management, in the purest sense, is taking the proactive and preventive approach of looking at everything to do with your Community—the area in which it is located and all the political, economic, environmental, and other factors that impact it—and then planning accordingly.

In a Community Association, when things go wrong or something outside the control of the Community occurs, there is no time for study and eventual recommendations. There is only time for action. Therefore, the Community should also be prepared with specific actions and responsible parties in case of emergencies, and as such, emergency preparedness should be treated as contingency management.

An emergency preparedness team should be established for your Community. Board members are mandatory members of the team. To build that sense of community, you can also generate an invitation to others in the Community to become a part of the team.

This is accomplished in two ways. First, in establishing the team, representatives from throughout the Community should be invited to join. This can be done by making a request for participants in your Association newsletter or as part of the agenda at the Board meeting. Make sure that you have as representative a group as possible.

Second, for those people who do not want to be members of the team, but who have input they want to provide, a request for that input should be made. This might be presented in the newsletter or in a mailing along with monthly assessments as follows.

*The Emergency Preparedness Team will soon be meeting to establish plans for the protection of our Community and its residents. In order to have the greatest levels of success, we need your help. We are looking for your ideas about issues and concerns that we should address. We will be addressing earthquake, fire, and other disaster safety plans, as well as pool and tennis court safety. If you have suggestions for other emergency or safety issues we should discuss, please submit them with your name, unit, and phone number to the Management Office. That way, we can put them on our agenda, and if we need information or clarification, we can contact you. Thank you for your help and support of your Community.*

The single largest component of your preparedness program is your *disaster plan*. The plan provides written details of what is to be done before, during, and after a disaster. A well designed plan can save lives, help emergency workers, and promote recovery. Very briefly, some of the elements of your disaster plan will include the following.

◆ An assessment of the disasters most likely to happen in your area and a list of measures that can be taken to mitigate damage in such disasters. (For example, securing artwork in common areas to keep it from falling during earthquakes, putting up brackets for easy installation of storm shutters, etc.)

◆ A complete list of residents, including children and pets, and each resident's emergency contact name and phone number. The list should make note of any individuals who might need additional assistance in an emergency. Also note residents who have special skills that might be useful in an emergency, such as doctors, nurses, EMTs, etc.

◆ Plans, drawings, or descriptions of all buildings within the complex, including the location of emergency exits, fire extinguishers, fire alarms, first aid kits, and other emergency supplies.

◆ A schedule showing when emergency equipment—such as extinguishers, alarms, and exit lights—is tested, and by whom. Regular drills should also be scheduled.

◆ A detailed emergency exit plan, showing safe routes for each area of the complex and including a place to meet outside of the building.

◆ An emergency phone list, including local hospitals, insurance company, board-up services, cleanup services, etc.

◆ The location of critical documents, such as insurance papers.

◆ A list of people other than residents who have keys to the facilities.

Along with the disaster plan, individual preparedness is critical. Most agencies recommend that individuals should be prepared to *shelter in place* for three days in case of a major emergency. That means having a disaster kit that can be used at home or in a shelter with a three-day supply of water, nonperishable food (including pet food), walking shoes, flashlight with extra batteries, extra eyeglasses, medications, copies of prescriptions, and a phone list, including family members, doctors, insurance agent, and an out-of-area emergency contact. Individuals should talk with their children's schools to find out what happens if there is an emergency during school hours. Also, people should talk with their veterinarian in advance to make arrangements for their pets in the event of a disaster.

Disaster preparedness is an ongoing commitment and education is another critical component. Education should be ongoing and it should involve all Community members, including children. Exit drills can help people prepare, and help them understand the potential for confusion and chaos during a disaster. Your Emergency Preparedness Team may want to establish a communication tree and a simple system of small groups of neighbors (three or four adjacent units) who will check on each other following a disaster.

A number of agencies can be extremely helpful as you prepare your disaster plan, develop individual awareness, and educate your Community residents. Local chapters of the American Red Cross offer cardiopulmonary resuscitation (CPR) and first aid training, as well as free disaster response training. The Red Cross website, **www.RedCross.org**, has detailed information on preparing for disaster for individuals, families, businesses, and communities. The Department of Homeland Security has a website that also offers planning advice at **www.ready.gov/america/make_a_plan.html**. In many communities, the fire department works with volunteers to create *community emergency response teams* (CERTs). Community emergency response team training prepares individuals to help in the immediate aftermath of a disaster. For more information, call your local fire department or go to **www.citizencorps.gov/cert**.

Unfortunately, many people do not start preparing for disasters until a disaster has already happened. Your Community Association's disaster planning is worth the time and effort it takes. It can safeguard your residents and help them cope with the unexpected—whatever form it takes. By making the whole Community a part of the preparedness process, there is a much greater likelihood that in the case of an emergency, everyone will come out of it better than could otherwise be expected.

## COMMUNITY SECURITY

As the population increases, and cities and towns grow larger, security becomes more important. Most Community Associations offer a degree of natural, mutual protection for residents living in close proximity, but residents watching out for each other may not be sufficient to protect and monitor the members and their property.

Unfortunately, video cameras, security guards, perimeter gates, patrol vehicles, and other components of a security system are becoming increasingly expensive. However, Community Association living makes it possible for members to enjoy security at a cost that is shared by all, lowering per-unit cost substantially when compared to the costs incurred by the owner of a house.

What should a Community do to establish a security system or evaluate a system that is in place? The following are some suggestions.

- Make a list of any vandalism, break-ins, or other crimes on Association property within the past three years.
- Confer with local law enforcement agencies to determine the crime rate in the area.
- Examine the geography, physical layout, and existing security to assess the Community's exposure to crime or vandalism.
- Ask other Associations or their management companies about what they are experiencing and what they are doing about it.
- Poll the owners in the Association about their experiences and their suggestions regarding security.

After determining the need for a security system and gathering some general ideas about establishing a system, move on to these steps.

- Invite local law enforcement agents to speak to the homeowners about security.
- Engage experts in the field to evaluate the Association's needs and give a presentation to Association members. (There could be costs associated with this step.)
- Seek referrals for security companies from local businesses and associations of a size comparable to your complex. (Make sure these security companies are not owned or operated by relatives or friends of those making the referral.)
- Invite several security companies to bid on a contract to provide security. Bids should include a list of references. Check on all references and check each company's reputation with local law enforcement. Bidders should be prepared to give a presentation to the Board and residents.
- Ask for an evaluation by your Association's insurance agent as to what kind of security system, if any, will result in savings on your premium.

While anyone who has been a victim of crime will quite naturally want the most aggressive form of security available, it may be equally effective to implement—and enforce—some security rules and to undertake more minor security measures. Some examples of these measures include the following.

- Contract with a graffiti-removal company that will apply protective coatings to vulnerable surfaces and remove graffiti immediately.
- Consider enforcing a system of fines for residents who block open common area doors and gates, such as those that give access to the hallways, garage, or street.
- Many complexes have one area that is more vulnerable to unwanted entry, such as a side gate or a wooded back perimeter. Consider improving security on that part of the property first.
- Intercom systems are of little security value if anyone can gain access by simply pressing buttons until someone lets them in. Instruct residents (and their visitors, guests, employees, and so on) to admit *only* people known to them.
- Residents must be vigilant when they are entering or exiting the complex, either in a vehicle or on foot. Once the door is open, it is easy for an unwanted visitor to slip in.
- Consider offering a brief class on personal security for residents. There are many very simple actions that can reduce the incidence of crime and its severity.

## PREFERRED SUPPLIER SYSTEMS

One of the most common mistakes made by Associations is using the same vendor or supplier over and over again simply because that is the person who has always done that work. It does not matter that the work is not done well or right the first time. You may even be aware that the technology the vendor is using is outdated or that you are being overcharged. Somehow the vendor still gets to keep the job.

The Association, like any successful business, must surround itself with the best possible suppliers for all its various needs in all regards. You would not want to work with an incompetent attorney or accountant. You also would not want an unqualified plumber working on your pipes.

The area of specialization is not at issue. What is at issue is that the Association must consciously and actively pursue developing a list of preferred suppliers who will give the best service at a competitive price when that service is needed.

It is even important that you stop thinking of the providers as vendors. That may be what they do, but to be a part of your Association's team, they must be considered preferred suppliers. As such, you must include your attorney, accountant, investment advisor, management company, plumber, gardener, and anyone else who is providing specialized services to the Association as part of your preferred supplier process and list.

By going through an objective selection process and carefully analyzing who will best serve your Community, you will be better able to strike the right deal with that provider. After all, this is a reciprocal relationship. You are giving these providers access to a revenue stream they did not have before. They must do their work well and work well with you to make sure that they keep that stream active.

Developing a list of preferred suppliers is not difficult. Once you have established a list of the expertise you require, take the following steps.

- Identify three to five reputable suppliers who can provide the service you need.
- Ask each to provide a bid or proposal for the job. Allow them adequate time for bid preparation. It can take up to a few weeks.
- Personally interview each supplier after receiving the bid. Ask such questions as the following.
    - Have they worked with Community Associations before?
    - Do they understand how decisions are made in the Association?
    - How long have they been in business?
    - What experience do they have with projects like the one on which they have bid?
    - Given their current and expected workload, when might your Association expect them to do the job requested?
    - What are their payment terms?

In addition, you will want them to provide you with documentation on their licensing, bonding, insurance, proof of or exemption from workers' compensation, and their safety record.

Once you have completed the interview process, selection of a preferred supplier will be easy. Also, keep in mind that in some cases, it is recommended that you have more than one supplier for the jobs the Community needs completed. In those cases, create a short list from those suppliers you interviewed with whom you want to keep in contact and give jobs as the need arises.

Some final points to consider as you look at your preferred supplier system include the following.

- Many homeowners do not know the difference between common areas that are the responsibility of the Association and those areas that are their responsibility. Make sure that when your suppliers are working on behalf of the Association, they are only doing work in common areas.
- Your Association may be able to establish a joint relationship with other Community Associations in the area. If you bid for jobs together, you can negotiate a better price.
- Some suppliers do not like working with Community Associations. If a vendor is not interested in working with your Association, do not worry. There will be others.

Remember that you are hiring your preferred suppliers for their expertise. Once you have them as part of your team, listen to their advice and input, and consider it seriously as you make your decisions.

Finally, regularly review your suppliers' work. Make sure that they are up to date, keeping their commitments, and working well with your Association. In some cases, you may even want to go through the selection process every few years to ensure that your Association is getting the very best knowledge and expertise available.

## ASSOCIATION OPERATIONS

There is a tendency to think that planning for or monitoring of Association operations is an almost impossible task. However, the information that the Board of Directors, Committees, management, and homeowners need can and should be readily available at any time it is requested.

There are four basic forms that, if used consistently and correctly, will give you the opportunity to adequately plan for and oversee the operations of your Association—whether you are the manager or a Board member overseeing activities. Each has a single purpose—to create visibility of the status of any given task or project in the Association.

The outcome of the use of these forms is simple, but central to the success of the Association. Use of the forms creates intense accountability. Whether it is a Committee's recommendation upon which the Board is waiting or an overview of the tasks that need to be accomplished each month for your preventive systems, those who are expected to perform know that expectation—and are held responsible and accountable for completing their task.

Over time, you may find that other forms are required. Again, determine what makes best sense for your Association and proceed accordingly. These forms will, at least, give you a start.

The four basic forms are:
1. Annual Overview Form
2. Action Item Form
3. Management Action Tracking Form
4. Committee Recommendation Form

Each is described in detail and a sample form of each is provided at the end of this chapter. While the forms are usable as they are presented, remember that it is important to customize any form to the specific needs and use of your Community. While you may decide to start with this version of the forms, keep thinking about how they might be improved for your purposes.

Finally, before going into the detailed explanations, a note on recordkeeping is important here. Recordkeeping is boring. No one likes to file or to make sure that there are adequate photocopies in the right place at the right time. It is tedious, unfulfilling, and generally left until the last moment. That moment, of course, usually occurs when you are desperately looking for a document that you have to have right now—and cannot find.

As you look at your planning and monitoring systems for Association operations, look at your recordkeeping systems as well. In some cases, you may be required by statute or your Association's own regulations to keep certain documents for a specified length of time.

Make sure that you keep copies of your annual budgets, annual reports, financial reports, balance sheets, minutes of all official Association meetings, tax returns, insurance papers, contracts, payroll, leases, warranties, permits, repair records, and other documents. You should also have original copies of all of your legal documents, including but not limited to CC&Rs, Articles of Incorporation, Bylaws, and condominium plans.

By taking care of your recordkeeping from the start, you will find your overall planning and monitoring process will be much easier to implement and maintain over time.

**Annual Overview Form**
The Annual Overview Form gives you a complete picture of the major tasks that need to be performed in all areas of your Community. It also provides you with the ability to see when those tasks are to be performed and by whom.

A sample of the form is on page 151. While it is a comprehensive form, it is simple to use. Just take the following steps.
- List the specific tasks that need to be performed in each of the major categories (i.e., Fiscal, Administrative/Clerical, Building Maintenance, Grounds Maintenance, and Miscellaneous).
- For each separate item on the list, mark the month or months during which the task is to be performed.
- In the last column, list the party responsible for completing that task (i.e., management, on-site employees, outside contractor, Board of Directors, or Association volunteers).

You will find that there can be four or five pages required to fully complete the form. That is fine. In the early stages of using the form, the more detail you have, the better. Eventually you may decide to cut back on the detail—but only after you have determined which items must remain and which can be incorporated into others. A copy of the form should be included in the Board Book every month, as well as posted in the manager's office for easy viewing.

## Action Item Form

The Action Item Form is the most important form used by your Association, and in particular, its management. The purpose of the form is to have an up-to-the-minute view of the specific tasks that are pending by management on behalf of the Association and homeowners.

When a homeowner submits a repair request to the manager, that task should immediately be put onto the Action Item Form so that it is visible to the manager as a constant reminder of those things that have yet to be completed.

A sample of the form is on page 152. The steps to complete the form are simple.

- ◆ Write the date that an action is requested or scheduled.
- ◆ Identify the person or party who is responsible for completing that task.
- ◆ Describe, specifically, what is required to complete the task. At the end, put a completion date.
- ◆ Mark when a task has been completed.
- ◆ If there are particular concerns about this task or necessary follow-up, add those in the final column.
- ◆ At the bottom of the page, remember to put the date that you begin using that particular page and the page number. Remember, this is a running account of what action items are still open, as well as those that are completed. Keep all of your pages as a record of your activities.

## Management Action Tracking Form

Each month prior to the Board meeting, the manager should take the Action Item Form open items, as well as any other open issues or projects, and compile them into an overview for the Board to review. The compiled information is reported on the Management Action Tracking Form.

Completing this form accomplishes two things. First, it allows the Board to clearly see the status on all open projects. Second, it demonstrates the progress the manager is making from month to month on behalf of the Association.

A sample of the form is on page 153. The following are the steps to take to complete the form.

- Mark the month and year for which this report is being compiled.
- Enter the date on which the original request was made or that the item appeared for the manager to address.
- Put a short description of the problem or issue that is being addressed.
- Identify the action or actions that need to be or are being taken.
- Note the deadline by which this project is to be completed.

You will note that deadlines play an important role in the planning and monitoring forms in the Association. This is not by accident. In general, unless a deadline is set for any task or project, it will not be completed.

Remember, intense accountability is the outcome of these forms. Assigned deadlines assist in providing that accountability and visibility.

## Committee Recommendation Form

To make things easier for the Board, as well as for legal purposes, Committees should provide a formal document with their recommendations for action to the Board of Directors. Those recommendations are described in the Committee Recommendation Form.

The form should be completed by the Committee chair with the active assistance of the other Committee members. In no cases should a chair or member be allowed to submit a Committee Recommendation alone. If a Committee member has an individual recommendation, that can be submitted on the Suggestion and Response Form, so as to not misrepresent where the recommendation comes from. (see Chapter 9, p.178.)

A sample of the form is on page 154. The steps to complete it are as follows.

◆ Identify the Committee, recommendation number (if any), the date the Committee agreed on the recommendation, and the submission date (if different).

◆ Describe the need that led to the Committee's addressing this issue.

◆ Provide a detailed description of the action(s) the Committee recommends should be taken by the Board.

◆ If there is a possible financial impact or cost to the Association, identify the amount, along with a recommended source of funding.

The last two sections are completed by the Board. Upon review of the Committee's recommendation, the Board should identify its decision or action taken, as well as any next steps that are requested—whether of the Committee, manager, homeowners, or other participant. The date that decision was made should be entered and the form should be signed by the Board Secretary.

Even after the Committee has completed the process and the Board has made the decision, this form should be kept with the Board minutes of the meeting during which the Board's decision was made.

Finally, to give the Board time to consider the recommendation before the Board meeting, it is recommended that the forms be submitted not less than one week prior to the scheduled Board meeting. If a form is turned in after that time, the issue should be tabled until the following month—unless the issue is so time sensitive that it absolutely requires immediate attention.

page ___ of ___        ___ (year)

## COMMUNITY ASSOCIATION
## ANNUAL OVERVIEW FORM

| Activity | Jan. | Feb. | Mar. | Apr. | May | Jun. | Jul. | Aug. | Sep. | Oct. | Nov. | Dec. | Responsible Party |
|---|---|---|---|---|---|---|---|---|---|---|---|---|---|
| **Fiscal** *(e.g., Budget Preparation, Financial Audit, etc.)* | | | | | | | | | | | | | |
| **Administrative/ Clerical** *(e.g., Annual Meeting, Welcome Packet Review, etc.)* | | | | | | | | | | | | | |
| **Building Maintenance** *(e.g., Inspection of Outside Contractor Performance)* | | | | | | | | | | | | | |
| **Grounds Maintenance** *(e.g., Landscape, Tennis Courts, etc.)* | | | | | | | | | | | | | |
| **Miscellaneous** *(e.g., Resales, Rentals/Leasing, etc.)* | | | | | | | | | | | | | |

## COMMUNITY ASSOCIATION ACTION ITEM FORM

| Date | Responsible Person or Organization | Action Required and Completion Date | Date Completed | Comments/ Follow-Up |
|------|------------------------------------|-------------------------------------|----------------|---------------------|
|      |                                    |                                     |                |                     |

Date: _____

Page _____ of _____

# Community Association

# Management Action Tracking Form

### Month/Year: _____

| Date of Request | Problem or Issue | Action Taken and Status | Deadline Date |
|---|---|---|---|
| | | | |

# Committee Recommendation
### (Submission Deadline is One Week Before the Board Meeting)

Committee: _____    Recommendation No.: _____

Date: _____    Submission Date: _____

**Description of Need:**

**Recommendation:**

**Financial Impact (including recommended source of funding):**

**Board Action and Requested Next Steps:**

Date: _____        _____
                                                    **Board Secretary**

# —9—
# COMMUNICATION AND MEETINGS

Throughout this book, the one constant is that if the communication within your Association is not adequate, the Association is guaranteed to have problems. In fact, the worse the communication, the more likely the problems will be big ones.

It is not just that information has to move. Appropriate information has to move to the right people at the right time, so that informed decisions can be made and the best actions for the Community can be taken. If the information is not there, the decisions and actions will be at risk.

Even more than that, if the communication is not good within the Association, the homeowners will not be able to feel like they are a part of a Community. They will feel as if they are paying into a large corporate entity with no knowledge whatsoever of what is being done with the money, whether their money is safe, or how well their property is being protected, preserved, and enhanced.

In simple terms, no communication means that the manager and Board are asking the homeowners to work on blind faith. That request is neither necessary nor fair.

When it is done right, communication creates community at all levels. Every person, because he or she is well informed, feels a part of something bigger and more important. This is particularly important for a Community Association, because every decision that is made impacts every person within the Community—homeowners, renters, and commercial tenants alike.

Oddly enough, communication breeds communication. If your Association is stingy about sharing information, just watch as you improve and expand your communication systems. You will see that as more information is available, more information is offered. Suddenly, you have more volunteers who want to help build the Community and work toward its needs. People feel part of something bigger and more important—making themselves feel even more important to the success of the larger Community.

Communication is an active and conscious task that requires attention. It is not difficult at all. However, real attention must be paid to making it the best communication for everyone involved.

Most communities share the same opportunities for communication. Those most common and important opportunities are:

- Board and Committee meetings;
- the annual meeting;
- Welcome Packets and Homeowner Manuals;
- newsletters; and,
- suggestion and response systems.

In addition, well-run Communities extend their information gathering and sharing to the larger community around them.

## BOARD AND COMMITTEE MEETINGS

Any meeting will be successful if it is well-managed—before, during, and after. After all, for the Board and Committees, each meeting both ensures completion of necessary tasks and introduces the next issues and tasks that need attention.

Once everyone knows the rules of how the meetings will be managed, it becomes simple to create success. The problem is that in most cases, either the meeting members do not know or do not care about the rules.

This is a particular challenge in Community Associations, as the Board and Committees are made up of volunteers. These people are already giving generously of their time—and they know it.

There are a lot of reasons for why homeowners decide to become actively involved in the oversight of the Association. The majority do so because they truly want to make their Community a better place to live. Some, however, do so because of the perks they think that they will get or deserve for giving their time. The perks range from expecting management to turn a blind eye to their little infractions of the rules and regulations of the Community, to actively seeking kickbacks from contracts they give to their friends and family members.

No matter what the case, well-run meetings will weed out the members with agendas and identify those homeowners who are interested in the good of the Community. This will ensure that the business that needs to be addressed is always at the forefront.

The rules for Board and Committee meetings are not difficult, but they must be followed consistently. Depending upon how detailed you want to become in setting up your rules, whole books have been written dedicated to successful meeting management in Community Associations. As a starting point, the following steps will make it easy to create and follow the rules for your Association.

## Step One: Before the Meeting

No meeting occurs in a vacuum. There had to be something that preceded the meeting that justified the meeting needing to take place. Even if this is the first time that your Board or Committee is getting together, there was a reason for that meeting to be scheduled in the first place.

The basis for the meeting is what determines your meeting agenda. In the case of Board and Committee meetings, the purpose of the meetings you hold is for decisions to be made and to monitor the actions taken on previous decisions.

The importance of meeting agendas cannot be overstated. They detail the expectations for the meeting and its participants, as well as provide the members with adequate warning about what they must be prepared to present or discuss.

Meeting agendas should be in the hands of the Board or Committee members one week prior to the scheduled meeting time. Further, all the documentation that is to be presented or reviewed should accompany the agenda. For Boards, this is called the *Board Book*. Most Committees do not have as formal a name for the materials, but the requirement is the same.

Committee agendas tend to be more simple and straightforward than Board agendas. For Committees, the various projects or tasks that they are reviewing or about which they are expected to make recommendations to the Board are on the agenda. If any new projects or tasks need to be added, those are listed as well.

For the Board, there are seven major agenda items that must be included at each meeting.

1. Review and approval of the minutes from the previous Board meeting.

2. Manager's Report—should include the Annual Overview and Management Action Tracking forms detailed in Chapter 8. (The Manager's Report is for update and status only. No decisions should be required, as the information being reported reflects the actions that have or are being taken on Old Business items that are now the manager's responsibility to complete.)

3. Treasurer's Report—should include a review of the Association's financial statements and status, as well as a discussion about reserve status and requirements.

4. Committee Reports—should be accompanied by the Committee Recommendation Forms that were submitted for the Board's review.

5. Old Business—includes the agenda items that have carried over from previous meetings. (Old Business agenda items are those that require decisions and about which additional information was required before the decision could be made. The item should have appeared as New Business in a previous agenda. At that time, for some reason the final decision could not be reached. The item is moved to Old Business because it is no longer new—even though it still requires a decision.)

6. New Business—includes new agenda items that require a decision by the Board before action can be taken. (Once the decision is made, the status is reported in the Manager's Report. If the decision cannot be made, usually because additional information is required, the item is moved to Old Business for the next meeting, at which point the decision should be made and action taken.)

7. Open Discussion and Question Period—gives homeowners who are in attendance the opportunity to address the Board with questions or issues they believe require attention.

To make the meeting run smoothly, your agenda should reflect who is responsible for presenting any particular information, as well as how long the participants will have to discuss that specific topic. That way, everybody knows what to expect of themselves and others.

Depending upon the complexity of your Association, you may want to have additional categories for your agenda, but those listed here will take care of the majority of the business requirements.

## Step Two: During the Meeting

Meetings, if not carefully managed, run amok. Homeowners ask questions when Board members are supposed to be discussing issues. Managers start asking for decisions during their report, even though the item is not even listed in the New Business agenda. Committee members do not have the information they were supposed to present and they blame their colleagues. Tempers fray, agendas are played out, and fists can fly.

What can you do to avoid this lunacy? From the beginning, create an environment of control and calm for your meeting.

In the first few meetings this may be more difficult, simply because people are not used to having their meetings carefully managed. That is okay. They will get the hang of it as long as you are consistent. Follow the agenda—exactly as it is shown.

If materials were supposed to have been included but were not sent in time, move the agenda item to the next meeting. If the person who was supposed to present gets angry, tough. He or she did not do his or her job. Do not let him or her get away with it.

Follow your time allocations. If a topic gets ten minutes, give it ten minutes. If more time is necessary, table the discussion until either the end of the meeting or the next meeting.

Start the meeting on time and end it on time. This is a sign of respect to all those who have made a point of arriving when they were supposed to. For those who came late, do not go back over material already covered. They were not there. They lose.

Do not be personal or take things personally. Inappropriate personal comments are simply not allowed.

If someone starts becoming disruptive, ask him or her to stop—and if he or she does not, tell him or her to leave. It does not matter who this person is. If individuals are that disruptive, they need to be out of the meeting. They can come back for the next meeting if they want, but with the understanding that they will behave. Remember that everyone involved is a grown-up and is expected to demonstrate at least basic good manners. If people refuse, they are out.

While the meeting is going on, the Secretary of the Board or Committee, the manager, or an outside administrative contractor specializing in meeting minutes should be taking notes. These are then turned into the formal meeting minutes.

As noted earlier, there are only four reasons for a Board of Directors to hold an executive session—to consider litigation; to cover matters relating to the formation of contracts with third parties; to consider discipline matters; or, to consider personnel matters. Any other discussions should be held in the regular sessions.

## Step Three: After the Meeting

Within forty-eight hours after the Board or Committee meeting, the Secretary should have generated and distributed the minutes for the meeting just held. By doing so, everyone has an opportunity to review what occurred while it is still fresh in their minds, and begin preparing for the next meeting.

Usually, upon reviewing the minutes, Board or Committee members will either have comments for the Secretary or want to suggest agenda items for the next meeting. Remember that any agenda items and their accompanying materials must be provided one week prior to the next meeting.

As for the minutes themselves, the important thing to keep in mind at all times is that minutes of meetings are discoverable. That means that in the case of litigation, the opposing attorney can ask for and receive the minutes of your Board or Committee meetings for the attorney's review. This also includes minutes for executive sessions.

Minutes are factual representations of the decisions and actions taken during the meeting. No personal comments should be included and there should be no editorializing. Issues are raised, decisions are made, and actions are taken. It is that straightforward.

Minutes are also a very good way for the Board to track how it and the manager are doing in running the Association. How many items keep reappearing in Old Business before a decision is made? How frequently are actions not completed on time and within budget? The minutes act as an assessment tool for the Board, Committees, and manager to determine not only how they can improve upon the meetings themselves, but more importantly, how the business of the Association can be improved.

## THE ANNUAL MEETING

The annual meeting is the bane of every Association's existence. Board members must have all of their information and documentation up to date to show exactly where the Association stands and how it has performed over the past year—as well as what needs to happen next. Candidates for available Board positions need to have submitted their information to be included on the ballot. Proxies must be included with the *Notice of Meeting*. The *Notice of Meeting* is required by the state and by your governing documents. Everything from what should be included along with the *Notice* to how far in advance it must be sent must be in compliance with both your state law and the requirements laid out in your governing documents. This is also why your team of experts needs to have provided all of their information for inclusion and report at the meeting.

Homeowners who have never been near a regularly held Board meeting suddenly appear not knowing the rules—and not caring. This, they believe, is their chance to air their issues about the Community, and they are going to take it.

In fact, the purpose of the annual meeting is a combination of legal requirements and the need to build community. From the legal standpoint, the annual meeting is the closest thing to a stockholder's meeting that an Association can hold. There are specific guidelines by law and in your Association's governing documents. You are best advised to work with your legal counsel in the setup and design of this meeting.

At the same time, you are trying to instill an even greater sense of community through the annual meeting. You want more people to become involved so that, eventually, you will have an even bigger selection of volunteers to hold future Committee and Board positions.

Even though it can get somewhat out of hand, you actually do want the input from the homeowners who show up only once a year and do not know the rules. Information is information—which means that the more you have, the better able you are to make decisions going forward. While their method of presentation might not be the best, the purpose at the heart of their comments is of value.

Because of the legal and Community-specific ramifications, it would be unfair and unrealistic for this book to present a complete guide to planning and running your annual meeting. Instead, and again with the recommendation that you work with your legal counsel, the following are some guidelines for you to observe.

- ◆ Put together a plan of action at the beginning of the year with specific dates by which tasks need to be completed and who will be responsible for each task.

- ◆ Make sure you follow your Association's and state's requirements regarding *Notice of Meeting* (particularly how far in advance it must be sent) and proxies.

- ◆ Know what constitutes a quorum for your Association.

- ◆ Have a sign-in table at the meeting at which people must stop before entering. They should either write their names or have them checked off of a comprehensive list of homeowner names by someone representing the Association. Proxies should be collected at the door.

- ◆ Establish the quorum before you can go forward. (The quorum is established by the combination of people attending and proxies submitted. If a quorum is not established to your state's or Association's satisfaction, the meeting must be rescheduled.)

◆ Give proof that there was a *Notice of Meeting* (usually by including a copy of the letter written on Association letterhead to each homeowner).

◆ Approve the minutes from the previous year's Annual Meeting. (These minutes should have been prepared and finalized by the then-existing Board within two weeks following last year's meeting. The minutes are held for approval until the next annual meeting.)

◆ Present the annual report of the Board and include a summary of the financial status of the Association, as well as reports by the Board President, Committee chairs, and management. (It is worth noting that since this may be the only time that many homeowners attend a meeting, the content should give the attendees the biggest bang for their buck. This may also get a greater level of participation in the ensuing year.)

◆ Determine through a resolution how excess funds will be allocated.

◆ Elect new Board members. Candidate information should have been distributed to the homeowners with the *Notice*—preferably three months before the meeting. The candidates are introduced and short speeches given by each. These speeches should be no more than two and one-half minutes each. There is no question and answer from the floor during or after these speeches—otherwise, your meeting will go on forever. If there are any nominations from the floor, this is the time to do so.

◆ Make sure that each unit gets only one vote by having people at the door double- and triple-check attendance against proxies. If a proxy has already been submitted and the homeowner decides to attend, tear up the proxy and hand the homeowner a ballot.

◆ Announce the results of the vote. (This is accomplished by the ballot counters giving a list of winners to the President, who then introduces the newly elected Board members.)

◆ Agree to a date for a joint meeting of the outgoing and incoming Boards. (This will assist in ensuring a smooth transition.)

◆ Adjourn the meeting.

Your Community Association may decide to combine the annual meeting with a social event. Although this is not necessary, it is worth considering. In the advance announcements of the meeting, promotion of social events, awards, door prizes, and food—and the promise of controversy—can contribute to greater participation and higher attendance numbers.

The main thing in your annual meeting is to be prepared for anything. Some Associations make sure that they have security visibly in attendance to offset the possibility of trouble. If you are on the Board or are a Committee member, be prepared to be frustrated by the questions people ask and the challenges they make to your work. Annual meetings, when well run, eventually create fair play. Again, in the early stages of putting your controls in place, everyone is learning the new rules.

## THE PURPOSE OF MINUTES

Minutes of meetings are vital to any business and are required for all corporations, including Homeowners Associations. The Secretary or a designated Assistant Secretary must sign the minutes, because the minutes then become the required evidence of the official acts of the Board.

If the minutes are signed by an unauthorized person or if there is no quorum, the subsequent meeting that has a quorum is the occasion for the chair to entertain a motion to ratify all lawful acts undertaken at the previous meeting or meetings. Any Board member may ask for such acts to be reviewed and move any specific act to be excluded from such ratification. This process allows business to proceed and prevents a minority from controlling things. If a previous Board has spent money or done anything improper, the act can be rescinded or the offending members may be liable to the Association.

Minutes are relatively easy to take, because brevity should be the rule. The Secretary should take general information as to the items of discussion, and detailed notes as to motions passed or failed and who made, seconded, and abstained in the vote. Minutes are the official record and are obtainable by owners and prospective buyers.

## Checklist for Conducting Meetings

❑ Always have an agenda, even if it is a single item meeting.

❑ Set a beginning and ending time, and begin precisely on time.

❑ One person must be in charge of the entire meeting, even though the management of the meeting may be delegated temporarily to others for reports and things of that kind. One person must always be perceived as being in charge.

❑ Make certain that every person at the meeting has an opportunity to ask questions, make comments, or contribute to the subject of the meeting.

❑ If someone attending the meeting is disruptive or causing problems, temporarily adjourn the meeting in order for tempers to cool and disruptive people to be taken away or otherwise dealt with, then resume the meeting.

❑ If possible, keep written handouts to a minimum, and make sure the materials are relatively easy to read and digest.

❑ If the meeting agenda deals with materials that have been distributed to the attendees before the meeting, all issues and questions pertaining to that material should be addressed in the time allotted for the meeting.

❑ Requirements for homeowners' conduct, including time limitations and placement on the agenda of their comments and questions, should be clear and as simple as practicable.

❑ Rules may require comments and questions to be in writing and submitted by a certain time prior to the meeting.

# Template for Meeting Minutes*

[Association's Letterhead]

[Month, day] 200___

## MINUTES OF  [BOARD OF DIRECTORS, EXECUTIVE SESSION, ANNUAL] MEETING

**Opening:**  [Time, date, place]

**Members present:** [Not necessary for Annual Meeting]

**Members absent:** [Authorized absence or not]

**Quorum:** [Yes/no]

**Previous Meeting Minutes:** [Approved or corrected/changed: moved and seconded by _____.] [Action Item]

**Treasurer's Report:** [Copy to be attached] [Approved/deferred: moved and seconded by _____.] [Action Item]

**Manager's Report:** [Copy to be attached] [Action Item]

**Committee Reports:** [Copy to be attached] [Action Items]
        Architectural
        Building and Grounds
        Financial
        Legal
        Social
        Ad Hoc (special area)

**Special Reports:** [copy to be attached] [Action Items]
        CPA
        Investments
        Reserve Consultants

**Homeowners:** Questions and comments [May be put in at any point in agenda] [Action Items]

**Unfinished Business:** [Action Items from past meetings]

**New Business:**

**Action Item List:** [To be acted upon by specific dates]

**Adjourned:**  [Time]

* This form may be helpful in preparing meeting agendas, but it can also be used as a template for minutes recorded by hand or on a computer during meetings.

# A NOTE ON PROXIES

For those meetings that require homeowner attendance and voting, a homeowner who is unable to attend may appoint someone to vote in his or her place. That appointment must be done with some formality, to control the number of votes. A *proxy* is the document that formally authorizes that appointment. In most cases, the right to accept votes by proxy is defined in the Association's documents, although the proxy form itself is seldom specified.

In general, Community Association voting by proxy is a privilege granted only to non-office-holding Community members. Officers and Board members may not have another Board member or officer vote in their stead. They must appear and vote in person or not be counted.

There are various kinds of proxies, but the one most commonly in use in Community Associations is the *general proxy*. A proxy can be issued for a particular voting event, such as an annual meeting, or for a specific or open-ended period of time when a number of votes may be called, such as a time when the proxy giver is on an extended vacation or otherwise unavailable. The general proxy directs the proxy holder to vote or to abstain from voting on all issues that come to a vote during the time specified by the proxy.

The advantage of a general proxy is that the vote of a missing homeowner can be counted. The disadvantage is that the person giving the proxy cannot tell the person holding the proxy how he or she should vote on any issue. If a controversial issue is likely to come to a vote, a proxy giver, under such circumstances, would be wise to give his or her proxy to someone who agrees with his or her point of view, because the proxy holder can vote his or her conscience.

You should consult your Association's documents to confirm any rulings regarding voting by proxy. A sample of a general proxy is included on page 168.

## Sample General Proxy

I, _____, being a member in good standing of the _____ [name of Association], do hereby appoint as my proxy holder _____ [name of proxy holder] to vote as he/she sees fit on all issues that may arise at the Annual Meeting [or other specified occasion] of the _____ _____ [name of Association] to be held on _____ [month, day, year] at _____ [time] at _____ [location]. This general proxy shall expire as of the time of the final adjournment of the Annual Meeting for which it is granted, unless sooner revoked by me.

Given this _____ day of _____, 20___.

_____
Printed name

_____
Signature

_____
Unit number

# WELCOME PACKETS
# AND HOMEOWNER MANUALS

One of the simplest and most straightforward ways of communicating with homeowners is to provide a *Welcome Packet* or *Homeowner Manual* to each new resident immediately upon their moving into your Community.

There is sometimes confusion as to whether there are multiple manuals or only one. The Welcome Packet, Homeowner Manual, or Rules and Regulations—whichever name your Association uses—is one document, preferably in a three-ring binder for easy update.

This manual should provide an overview of the rules and regulations of the Association along with helpful information that will make the residents' transition into Community members easier.

Welcome Packets should not be confused with the CC&Rs, Bylaws, and other governing documents of the Association. While each homeowner must be provided with copies of those, the Welcome Packet or Homeowner Manual is a friendlier, more easy to use compilation of useful information.

The manual needs to be reviewed and revised regularly. There is a tendency to ignore the manual once it has been written—and only when it becomes embarrassingly out of date does the Board take on the responsibility for updating it. Instead, an annual review of the contents should be made either by the Board or by the Communications Committee. The Committee would then be responsible for doing the update and presenting the text to the Board for review.

The contents of the manual are usually straightforward. While each Association will be different, some basic components should be expected. They are:

- a table of contents at the beginning, providing a complete list of the topics covered and on which page;
- a letter of welcome from the Board of Directors to new residents to the Community;
- a section on rules and regulations listing formal and informal rules, including information on enforcement, due process, and conflict of interest (other policies, such as those related to fee payment, use of contractors, renters and guests, parking, and pets should also be included);

- Board and Committee information (including a list of Board members and their contact information, Committee names and chair contact information, dates of regularly scheduled Board and Committee meetings, the policy on attendance at Board meetings by homeowners, and information on how to become involved as a volunteer, along with any other relevant information);
- an overview of legal and financial information (including information on state or local laws and provisions that must be known to the homeowners, along with a copy of the annual budget, information about fees, dues, fines, assessments, and assessment policies included in the same or in its own section);
- comprehensive information about your management (especially contact information), security, security systems that include key and code management for homeowners, management, vendors, emergency procedures (including the emergency preparedness team members), facilities and common area information, a map of the premises, local services, and a calendar of events other than Board and Committee meetings; and,
- a copy of the Suggestion and Response Form (see page 178) and any other standardized forms used by the Association, along with submission information.

After you have published your first manual and have information on the types of questions that are most frequently asked, you may want to add a Frequently Asked Questions (FAQ) section. Depending upon the needs of your Association and how quickly things change, the FAQs may need to be updated annually. If this is the case, work with your management to determine whether it makes sense to include that section or if they prefer to continue fielding questions directly in the management office.

These materials, which are subject to change, are valuable to homeowners. Updated copies of any materials that change or need special emphasis can be handed out at the annual meeting.

In preparing your materials, put the emphasis on *easy access to information*. Do not make readers wade through paragraphs of narrative if a few bullet points will do. Avoid legal jargon and formal language in favor of straightforward, simple writing. Make sure a revision date appears at the bottom of every sheet. A consistent page layout will make your packet look more professional.

Though your association's size, location, and population will determine the specific contents of your Welcome Packet, the following is a checklist of some general suggestions for materials to include.

### Checklist for New Resident Welcome Packet

❏ Table of contents.

❏ Letter of welcome from the Board of Directors.

❏ Rules and regulations, both formal and informal. Established Association policies regarding use of contractors, conflict resolution, renters, guests, architectural standards, parking, pets, noise, home businesses, insurance claims, trash, and so on.

❏ Overview of legal and financial information. Relevant state or local laws, the annual budget, information about fees, dues, fines, assessments, and assessment policies. The financial plan for reserve funds and investments belongs here as well.

❏ Board and Committee information. A definition of the role of the Board and its officers; the Board meeting schedule; the policy on attendance by Association members; a list of recurrent tasks handled by the Board; and, a list of names, titles, and phone numbers for current Board members and Committee chairs. Describe how residents can get involved with Committees and provide a form to make it easy for them to do so.

❏ Management and outside services. A list of names and numbers for professional services used by the Association, including management company, accountant, legal counsel, security service, architect, bank, insurance company, gardening, pest control, general maintenance, pool, and heating and air conditioning.

❏ Security. General security practices, plus phone numbers for neighborhood watch, security patrol, and local police.

❏ Emergency. A set of recommended guidelines for actions in preparation for, during, and after an emergency. Put the emphasis on fire and the other most common local emergencies. Include contact information for emergency preparedness team members.

❏ Facilities. A list of all the common area recreational facilities—pool, spa, tennis court, gym, recreation room, etc.—including location, hours, and rules of operation. Also, include services available to residents—valet, door service, salon, massage, etc.—and contact phone numbers.

❏ Newsletter. Include a copy of the two most recent issues. If you accept photos, articles, or other input from residents, include a submission form.

❏ Calendar. If your Association schedules events in addition to Board meetings, include a calendar.

❏ Map. A map of the grounds—even for the smallest condominium building—can be helpful to the new resident. Include the location of important switches, meters, and emergency exits.

❏ Local services. Nearby services—especially those that deliver or stay open all night—are a useful addition to your welcome packet. Include pharmacies, restaurants (you may even want to include menus), dry cleaners, transportation (taxi, bus, etc.), and libraries.

❏ Important information. If your Association maintains office copies of keys, codes, or emergency contact information for residents, provide an easy form for residents to complete.

❏ Frequently Asked Questions. Take a hint from the Internet and include a list of FAQs with their answers.

❏ Suggestions. Association residents may have suggestions for additions or changes to your Welcome Packet or other Association concerns. If you provide a suggestion form and a suggestion box, residents will feel more involved in the welfare of the Association.

## Welcome Letter for New Resident

Dear _____ [new resident's name],

We are so pleased to welcome you to _____
[name of complex or Association], and hope that you will be happy
living here for many years to come.

    As a new resident, you will undoubtedly have questions. You
should have already received a Homeowner Manual, which contains
many important documents. Attached to this note is your Welcome
Packet, in which you will find all kinds of useful information, and
probably the answers to many of your questions. Of course, if you
have additional questions, please give me [or name of manager/staff
person] a call and we will be happy to help you find the answers.

    One of the reasons that _____
[name of complex or Association] is such a great place to live is that
so many of our neighbors participate in Association Committees and
activities. Your involvement is not only beneficial to our Community,
but it is also a great way to get to know people. We hope you will use
the enclosed Committee Interest form to select an activity or two and
leave your completed form in the Manager's office.

    We look forward to getting to know you and to helping you get
settled in _____ [name of complex or Association].

Yours sincerely,

_____

[signature]

# NEWSLETTERS

Newsletters are the easiest and most efficient means an Association has for sharing information and building a sense of Community. Newsletters set a tone for the Community—that the Board and management are interested in what the Community has to say and want to keep them informed.

Your newsletter does not have to be long—and it should not be. Some of the most successful newsletters are only one page and are sent out each month along with the assessment invoices. This ensures that every homeowner gets a copy, and has a quick update on the items of interest and importance to the Community. Copies of the most recent newsletter should also be available in the management office.

In designing your newsletter, be creative. Give it a good name that catches people's attention. With computer graphics being as simple as they now are, design the logo so that it is colorful and eye-catching.

Set out your headlines so that each article's intent is clear. You may want to look at your favorite newspaper or magazine to see what it is that they do that works so well for you.

Make the articles short and direct. Edit your content so that the first paragraph gives the most information—after all, many of your readers will never go beyond those first lines. Paragraphs and sentences should be kept short, and avoid using jargon that is not commonly understood.

Include graphics and photos wherever possible. This makes your newsletter more interesting and allows people to get a snapshot of information that they can use. Also, make sure you use an easily readable and large enough font. There is nothing more frustrating than having to squint to read a document.

Your newsletter should be personal and specific to your Community and its needs. The Board President should write a message to the Community in each issue and the Committees should have a quick update of their activities. Meeting schedules and events should be provided, as well as requests for participation by new volunteers.

If this is your first issue, the President should write a welcome letter that describes some of the exciting changes and innovations, and invites people to become a part of the larger Community. For example, it may read as follows.

*Welcome to our first monthly newsletter. I am glad to have this opportunity to speak to all the Community residents about the positive and exciting changes our Association has in store this year.*

*I am committed to making the Association work to all of our benefit. For this year, that means that one of the Board's primary focus areas will be to make the business of the Association all the more successful.*

*Our management and Board members have brought our Community to a higher level of efficiency and effectiveness than ever before. It is now time for us to build upon and expand those successes.*

*Some of the changes will be easy to see. For example, this newsletter. The purpose of the newsletter is to assist in building a greater sense of Community—to make it possible for all homeowners to know what is going on and participate to as great an extent as possible.*

*Our manager and the Communications Committee will be doing all they can to make sure that the newsletter works as a positive communication tool for all of the residents. Also, by including the newsletter with the monthly bills, we make sure that everyone has the opportunity to get the same information at the same time.*

*Further, the Social and Communications Committees will be working jointly to design and then invite all residents to social functions at least four times yearly. We will also be updating the Homeowners Information Packet to ensure that all homeowners— both new and long-time residents—have the most up-to-date information possible about the Association and the Community.*

*Our Association is both a business and a Community. In effect, the Association is the business of the Community. I look forward to working with you all in making this both the best and the most successful Community possible.*

As always, the text should be customized to your Association's needs. Just keep the tone positive and forward-looking, and you will achieve the goal you have set.

# SUGGESTION AND RESPONSE SYSTEMS

No organization of any type can rest on its laurels. Improvement must be a constant goal for the Community in all its areas of operation. To that end, a suggestion system is key to the long-term success of the Community and its Association.

Suggestion systems have gotten a bad name over the years—mostly because people submit their suggestions and then nothing happens. The way to ensure that homeowner suggestions are taken seriously is to develop a suggestion and response system.

The sample Suggestion and Response Form on page 178 demonstrates how, by making the system reciprocal and accountable, homeowners can be assured that their ideas are not being ignored or wasted.

The steps to complete the form are as follows.

- ◆ Write your name clearly in the space provided, along with your unit number and the date that you are submitting your suggestion. This is very important, as you will be contacted for additional information if necessary. If no name or unit number is provided, the suggestion may not be considered or an action may not be taken.

- ◆ In the top box, write your question, suggestion, or comment. Do not write angry or inappropriate comments. Do not swear or insult anyone or anything to do with the Community. Instead, put down your thoughts and concerns clearly and concisely, so that they can be given due consideration.

- ◆ Make sure, in providing your input, that you note whether you believe that there are any legal or financial risks to the Association by continuing with the current state of affairs. Also, do not just complain. Include your ideas or suggestions for action. This will give the responding party a head start on being able to address the issue.

- ◆ After you have completed the form, return it to the management office. If the question requires attention from the Board of Directors, the form should be submitted at least one week prior to the next scheduled Board meeting.

- ◆ Once the manager has your completed form, he or she will take appropriate action. Depending upon your concern or suggestion, it may be something that needs to move to a Committee, be handled by an outside contractor or expert, or be solved by the manager him- or herself. Whatever action is taken, the manager should write that information down and ensure that you are given a photocopy of the completed form.

It is management's responsibility to ensure that each homeowner receives a response as quickly as possible—definitely no later than immediately following the next Board meeting. By doing so, homeowners know that they are being heard, and management knows that it is responsible and accountable for taking action on suggestions that are submitted.

The manager may even want to include a quarterly update at the Board meetings as part of his or her Management Action Report. This update should note the number of suggestions received, the outcomes of those suggestions, and any cost savings to the Community or other benefits realized from the program.

In addition to suggestion boxes and suggestion forms, your Association might want to circulate an annual questionnaire seeking resident feedback. The questionnaire might ask for a rating or evaluation (excellent, good, fair, poor) of Association services, maintenance, and management. It can informally poll residents on questions that have come before the Board (for example, whether the residents would be in favor or opposed to using the area adjacent to the maintenance shed for a vegetable garden), it can ask for feedback on newsletters and décor, and it can solicit additional suggestions and comments from residents. The results of the questionnaire can be published in the newsletter, and suggestions can be submitted for additional study and consideration.

As you will soon see, when homeowners realize that attention is being paid to their suggestions, the number of good, substantive suggestions will grow quickly. This creates yet another way of preserving, protecting, and enhancing your Community and your home.

## Community Association
## Suggestion and Response Form

Your name: _____

Unit number: _____
Date: _____

Please write your suggestion, question, or comment in the space below, and return this form to the manager's office. Questions for the Board of Directors must be submitted at least one week prior to the Board meeting.

Manager: Please note the action taken and response given to the homeowner in the space below.

# BEING PART OF THE LARGER COMMUNITY

Finally, as you look at your communication with and contribution to your immediate homeowner Community, you should also be aware of the importance of taking your place within the larger community. Whether your Community is surrounded by office buildings or in a rural area far away from the city lights, your relationship with your local government is crucial to the long-term success of your Association.

Police, fire, and utility departments, as well as others have special offices dedicated specifically to providing services to Communities and Community Associations. These departments have valuable information for you and your Community that will ensure your safety.

You should become involved in your local city council, attend meetings, and be aware of the issues confronting your immediate area. After all, the decisions being made for single family homes and apartment renters can have just as big an effect on your Community, and in some cases, more so.

Quite often, city decisions can impact the finances of your Community. Decisions regarding laws and regulations in your area should take into consideration the very special needs of Communities such as yours. If such laws are implemented without your input or knowledge, your Association can find itself paying fines for which it was not prepared.

Community Associations have great influence in the greater community. In one limited area, you represent a much larger percentage of homeowner population than in a comparable single family home area. Importantly, because you are homeowners, you pay taxes not paid by renters. Your Community should use its influence to ensure that the people who make decisions receive input regarding public utilities, zoning, stores, restaurants, parks, schools, and other facilities utilized by you and your neighbors.

Be smart about becoming a part of the larger community. Just as you do not want homeowners who are not knowledgeable about the workings of the Community complaining at Board meetings, you should make yourself knowledgeable about the workings of your local government and the issues it is addressing. Participate at meetings—first as an observer, and eventually, as an active participant.

Make yourself known to local officials—particularly letting them know that you are a part of your Community and its Association. If you are the Board President or a Committee chair, make sure that they know the position you hold.

Volunteer to assist the local area officials and neighborhood groups in their projects and task forces. Keep them apprised of your Community's activities by sending them copies of your monthly newsletter. You may even want them to come speak about a particular issue at one of your Board meetings or special events.

When you speak, speak with assurance and with the facts behind you. Make sure your local officials know that you really understand what you are talking about.

Do not be argumentative or demeaning toward government employees. These are the people who are trying to help you. As you make it clear that you, too, are committed to achieving their goals for the community, you will find yourselves working in concert and toward an acceptable consensus.

Beyond your local government, you should also become involved with the local chapter of Community Associations Institute (CAI) or other national Community Association organizations. Your state or local area may also have organizations specifically committed to Community Associations.

Find out what organizations are meeting and when. Get copies of their publications, attend meetings, and speak with other Community Association Board or management members from your area. Be involved. The more that you gain and share information, the better it will be for your Community.

## Committee Interest Form

Please use this form to indicate your interest in participating in one or more of the _____ [name of complex or Association] Committees.

Date _____

Name _____

Unit _____

Telephone _____

Email _____

I would like to participate in the following Committees:

_____ Architectural

_____ Building and Grounds

_____ Finance

_____ Legal

_____ Maintenance

_____ Newsletter

_____ Recreation

_____ Rules

_____ Social

_____ Welcoming

_____ I am OR _____ I am not willing to serve as chair of a Committee.

The best time for me to attend meetings is ____ days ____ evenings ____ weekends ____ any time.

I am willing to share my skills in the following areas with the Association:

_____ Event Planning

_____ Writing

_____ Design/Decoration

_____ Accounting/Finance

_____ Other (please list) _____  _____

We appreciate your interest and welcome your participation. Please leave the completed form in the manager's office and you will be contacted by a Committee representative.

# –10–
# A FINAL NOTE: YOU AND YOUR ASSOCIATION

Simply by reading this book you have already demonstrated your commitment to your Community and your Association. By now you may have even begun attempting to implement some innovations and new ways of thinking into your Board, Committee, and management operations.

This is the point at which you need to remind yourself that just because you have this better understanding of what can be and what needs to be done to achieve those goals, does not mean everyone else sees what you see. In fact, in most cases, it will take quite a bit of time until others see what you see.

One of the most frustrating aspects of Community Association improvement is that one voice begins the process. Remember, you have taken the time to learn about your Association. Part of that learning is the understanding that it took a number of years to get the Association to the point it is at now—both the good and the bad—and it will take a few years to get it where it needs to go.

The problems that are most apparent to you will become apparent to most of your Community members quickly. They will see that, in fact, major improvements have been put off and must be done now. They will start asking questions about the Association's finances in particular, since that has the most direct impact on their households. The biggest, most threatening problems confronting your Association will most likely be taken care of relatively soon.

Over time—during which you should plan to feel frustrated—people will begin seeing some of the things you see, but usually not with the same level of insight that you demonstrate. As they gain this understanding, the improvements will not only occur, but will be integrated into how the Association operates.

In effect, the time it takes to get people to truly see what the Association can and will be—with their help—also allows the Community to ensure that the problems that occurred will not occur again.

Some people will start asking you how you learned all you now know. Few will want to pursue the same self-education process that you have pursued, but you should expect to be treated as the Community's resident expert in all things to do with the Association.

Sometimes you will want to move faster than the Community is able to move. If that presents a big enough problem, you may have to think about moving away. This is not the same as running away. It is a realistic look at the state of your Association and the impact for your home, property, and investment. If your Association summarily refuses to make the much needed improvements that will ensure that your property value is maintained and improved, you simply cannot afford to stay.

Look at what you are doing—and the response you are getting—objectively, and then make your determination. Some Associations are doomed to fail. It is not any one person's fault. It is a combination of history and a refusal to take the actions necessary to reverse the current situation. If your Association is pointing in that direction, you are best served leaving before the Association goes bankrupt than staying and being just as affected as your neighbors.

As you become more involved in your Association, you may find yourself taking on more and greater responsibilities. It does not matter if you had never intended to become a Board member. If you need to do so to effect the changes necessary, do it. It will do you and your Community good. It will also give you a bird's-eye view of the real state of the Association. It may be through just such an intervention that you stop a downward spiral for the Community and its Association that would have negatively impacted everyone.

Sometimes the problem lies in the lack of cooperation between the Board—particularly the Board President—and management. There is an interesting concept in business called *synergy*. The word *synergy* is a combination of the words *synthesize* and *energy*. Basically, it means putting two seemingly different parts together to create a greater outcome than either would be able to achieve alone.

This synergy must be created and maintained between the manager and the Board. They are both on the same side—looking out for the Association and all its Community members. Each has a particular responsibility, which, when combined, make the Community the best possible place to live.

From the time you become involved in the Association, make a point of working cooperatively and collaboratively with management. Their success is your success. After all, if they get the reputation of having worked with a Community that failed, it will do real damage to their future employment prospects. They want you to succeed as much as you do.

Over time, assess whether you really are best suited to a Community living situation. The fact is, some people are not suited to Community living. People often move into Community situations because condominiums or townhomes are less expensive than single family homes. They do not, however, always understand what it takes to successfully live in such a Community.

Community living requires always looking at the greater good. Nothing outside your door is specific to your particular home. Everything to do with your property impacts everyone else, and vice versa.

As you continue to work with your Community to make it better, always keep in mind that you live in a shared community. It is not just that you share walls with your immediate neighbors. It is that you share a common environment that provides you with an immediate community—of which you are an important part.

Take the opportunity to contribute all that you can to your Community and its greater good. By doing so, you will make your and your Community members' living situations go far beyond shared walls.

# GLOSSARY

## A

**accounting.** System of gathering financial information and keeping a record of business transactions to prepare statements concerning assets, liabilities, and operating results.

**accrual accounting.** Method of recording expenses incurred and income due in the periods to which they relate rather than actual flow of cash.

**additional insured.** Person or entity added to an insurance policy as an insured, such as a mortgagee, lessor, or subcontractor.

**ad hoc committee.** Special Committee that is appointed to carry out a specific, nonrecurring task and is disbanded when that task is completed.

**agenda.** Sequence in which issues are to be taken up in a meeting.

**airspace.** Space located within or above the boundaries of the property that is sometimes owned by the individual members in common, or by the Association.

**all-risk insurance.** Policy under which a loss resulting from any cause other than those causes specifically excluded by name is considered to be covered.

**alternate dispute resolution (ADR).** Methods of resolving disputes other than by judicial process, including mediation and arbitration.

**amend.** Modify or change. Under parliamentary procedure, you can modify a motion by adding, deleting, or substituting words.

**amendment.** Revision of a governing document, or under parliamentary procedure, a motion.

**annual membership meeting.** Once-a-year assemblage of unit owners, required by governing documents to conduct Association business, such as electing a Board of Directors.

**annual report.** Report given once a year by the Board to the membership showing the condition of the Association fiscally and otherwise.

**answer.** Pleading filed by a defendant or respondent, setting out the reasons why the relief sought in a complaint or petition should not be granted.

**arbitration.** Form of litigation wherein one arbitrator (or often three arbitrators) constitute the tribunal, where evidence is offered and a decision or award is made in favor of the winning party; no negotiation is involved as to the substantive issues of the matter.

**arbitration award.** Final written decision of the arbitrator or arbitrators.

**articles of incorporation.** Formal document that, when filed, sets up an Association as a corporation under the laws of the applicable state.

**assessment.** Amount charged against each unit owner based on percentages of budgeted common expenses to fund the operation, administration, maintenance, and management of the Community.

**audit.** Examination of inventories, insurance policies, management, and financial records and accounts to verify their accuracy and determine if they adequately reflect an Association's status.

**auditor.** Person or firm, usually accountants, engaged to examine financial documents for errors or fraud.

# B

**balance sheet.** Financial statement that indicates the financial status of an Association at a specific time, listing its assets, liabilities, and members' equity.

**ballot.** Paper used to cast secret vote.

**bid invitation.** Invitation sent out to vendors to bid on providing services or equipment of a substantial nature.

**billing.** Written statement showing the work done by a vendor for goods or services in such detail as to accurately describe the basis for each charge.

**binding arbitration.** Arbitration that is final with no further recourse at the trial level. Arbitration is presumed to be binding unless there is some contrary provision in the contract providing for arbitration.

**board book.** Documents compiled, reported, and reviewed each month by management and Board members for discussion and decision at regularly scheduled Board meetings.

**board of directors.** Official governing body of a Community Association, elected by members of the Association.

**budget.** Estimated summary of expenditures and income for a given period.

**business judgment rule.** Standard of conduct for the Board of Directors; also called the prudent person rule.

**bylaws.** Secondary laws of an Association that govern its internal affairs and deal with routine operational and administrative matters.

# C

**California Association of Community Managers (CACM).** Professional trade organization offering a statewide certification program.

**capital expenditures.** Funds spent for additions or improvements to a physical plant or for equipment.

**cash accounting.** Method of recording revenue when actual cash is received and expenses when actual cash disbursements are made.

**certified public accountant (CPA).** Accountant who has met certain state legal requirements.

**committee.** Group of people officially designated to perform a function, such as investigate and report on a matter to the Board of Directors.

**common areas.** Property owned jointly by all unit owners that ordinarily includes land and structure or portions of structure not otherwise described as units.

**common expenses.** Costs of managing, maintaining, administering, repairing, replacing, and operating the Community.

**common interest development (CID).** Community Association in the form of condominiums, stock cooperative, community apartment project, or planned development.

**community apartment project.** Development where an undivided interest in the land and the building is tied to the exclusive right to occupy an apartment. This means that the owners of the development, through the Association, are their own landlords.

**community association.** Private organization, usually nonprofit, responsible for the total operation of communities, including but not limited to condominiums, cooperatives, time-shares, and planned unit developments.

**Community Associations Institute (CAI).** Independent nonprofit research and educational organization formed in 1973 to develop and distribute guidance to condominium and Homeowners Associations.

**complaint.** Pleading filed by a plaintiff or petitioner setting out the reasons why relief should be granted.

**conditions, covenants, and restrictions (CC&Rs).** In some jurisdictions, a basic document recorded to enumerate the property interests in a Community Association, similar to a Declaration.

**condominium.** Form of ownership in a multifamily housing development that combines exclusive ownership of a dwelling unit and joint ownership of common areas.

**conflict of interest.** Situation in which a person has two or more interests that conflict.

**contingency.** Event that may occur, but is not necessarily expected.

**contingency fee.** Fee paid to a lawyer consisting of a percentage of the amount recovered in litigation.

**contingency reserves.** Funds set aside to cover unanticipated emergencies or major expenditures not included in the current fiscal year operating budget.

**contract.** Voluntary and legally binding agreement between parties calling for them to do or not do some specific thing for some consideration, usually monetary.

**cooperative.** Corporation that holds real estate, specifically a multifamily dwelling, in which shareholders have the right to live in one of its units; also called a co-op.

# D

**declaration.** In some jurisdictions, this is a basic document recorded to set out property interests in a Community Association, similar to CC&Rs.

**deductible.** Specific amount to be subtracted from a loss and written into an insurance policy as a means of effecting a decrease in premium.

**default.** Failure to fulfill or live up to terms of an agreement.

**deferred maintenance.** Upkeep that may be scheduled at a future date without allowing a minor problem to become a major one.

**delinquency.** Overdue assessment payment.

**directors and officers liability insurance (D&O).** Protection against loss arising out of alleged errors in judgment, breaches of duty, and wrongful acts of a Board of Directors and officers in carrying out their prescribed duties.

**discoverable documents.** Documents that may be required to be produced in the discovery phase of litigation.

**due process.** Concept of fundamental fairness, such as the right to reasonable notice to present evidence and cross-examine witnesses at a fair and impartial tribunal.

# E

**early neutral evaluation.** Neutral party brought into a dispute to evaluate it for possible resolution before litigation is begun.

**easement.** Right to use land owned by someone else for certain limited purposes, such as for party driveways, drainage, and so on.

**emergency maintenance.** Necessary repairs that cannot be predicted and that require immediate attention.

**enforcement.** Association action in applying the appropriate penalties for violating its rules.

**equity.** Owner's interest in a property, usually determined by the value of the property less mortgage, liens, or other encumbrances against it.

**equity accrual.** Buildup of an owner's interest in a property because of mortgage loan amortization or appreciation in its total value.

**errors and omissions insurance (E&O).** Protection against loss arising out of an alleged error or oversight on the part of an insured professional while performing prescribed duties.

**estimated budget range.** Item in a budget that is not certain, so an estimated amount is used, generally based upon the amount in the prior budget and other pertinent considerations, such as possible increases or decreases in revenue and expense expectations.

**evaluative mediator.** Mediator who injects an opinion or evaluation into a mediation.

**evidentiary hearing.** Hearing where evidence is used by the tribunal to make a decision of liability or fault, such as an arbitration or trial.

**expenses.** Costs incurred by the Association for its operations.

**external legal issues.** Legal conflicts that arise between the Community Association and outsiders.

# F

**facilitative mediator.** Mediator who facilitates the conclusion of a mediation without expressing an opinion as to the mediation issues.

**Federal Housing Authority (FHA).** Federal agency that functions as an insurer of mortgage loans.

**fiduciary duty.** Responsibility of the Board to exercise a high degree of care in acting for the financial benefit of the members rather than for themselves; also called fiduciary responsibility.

**fiduciary relationship.** Agreement based on trust in which one person or group of persons handles financial transactions for another or others.

**financial management.** Management of the day-to-day affairs of a Community Association's financial issues, such as whether or not certain revenue or expenses are within the budget.

**financial statement.** Report that indicates certain information concerning the financial position of an Association.

**fiscal controls.** Procedures for regulating and verifying the financial activities of an Association.

**fiscal year.** Twelve-month period for which an Association plans use of funds.

**fixed expenses.** Costs that remain relatively stable.

**fraud.** Deliberate deception practiced to secure unlawful gain.

**fundamental fairness.** Conduct by one to others that is in keeping with the simple and basic ideas of what is fair treatment.

# G

**general maintenance.** Upkeep that can be anticipated and performed on a regular basis, or that is minor in nature.

**governing documents.** Set of legal papers, filed by a developer with the appropriate local government office, that submit land to use for, create, and govern a Community Association.

**grandfathered.** Amendment to a governing document that changes rights or restrictions while preserving an owner's rights who relied on the documents at the time of purchase.

# H

**hearing.** Examination, usually informal, of an accused person.

**heating, ventilation, air-conditioning system (HVAC).** The unit regulating the even distribution of heat and fresh air throughout a building.

**homeowners association.** An organization of homeowners whose major purpose is to maintain and provide for the rights of owners.

**house rules.** Guidelines related to day-to-day conduct in common areas and relationships between unit owners.

# I

**income tax.** Charge levied by the federal government against taxable income of an individual or corporation.

**indemnification.** Condition, usually contractual, of being protected against possible damage, loss, or suit.

**injunctive relief.** Court order that grants a petition for the mandate or prohibition of conduct or acts by a person or entity.

**insurance.** Protective measure that shifts risk of financial loss due to certain perils to an insurance company in return for payment of premiums.

**insurance agent.** Representative of an insurance company, licensed by the state, who negotiates and effects insurance contracts, and also services policyholders.

**insurance broker.** One who shops around with many insurers as the agent of the insured.

**insurance claim.** Sum of money demanded for a loss in accordance with the terms of an insurance policy.

**insured.** One covered by insurance; a policyholder.

**insurer.** One who provides insurance; an insurance company.

**interest.** Charge for a financial loan, usually based on a percentage of that loan.

**internal legal issues.** Legal conflicts that arise between owners, or between an owner and the Community Association.

**investment.** Outlay of money to realize income or profit in the future.

**investment summary.** An attachment to the periodical financial summaries of operations that indicates the amount of investments held, the institution where invested, the rate of interest, and the maturity date (where applicable).

# J

**judgment.** Court decree of indebtedness to another and amount of that indebtedness.

# K

**kickback.** Improper payment in cash, goods, or services to one who holds an official position, made in order to influence that person.

# L

**legal oversight.** Responsibility of the Board to engage outside legal counsel to advise it on legal matters.

**liability.** Legal responsibility and obligation.

**liability insurance.** Coverage for damages arising out of an insured person's legal responsibility and resulting from injuries to other persons or damage to their property.

**lien.** Claim or attachment, enforceable at law, to have a debt or other charge satisfied out of a person's property.

**limited common areas.** Property that physically is part of a Community Association's common areas, but is reserved for the exclusive use of a particular unit owner or group or unit owners.

**line item budget.** Format of listing expenses by type.

**litigation.** Any proceeding wherein each party submits evidence and a tribunal decides the issues in dispute, such as an arbitration, trial, or appeal.

**loss.** Amount of an insured's claim; amount of decrease in value of the insured's property.

# M

**maintenance.** Upkeep of property or an item in its proper and functional condition.

**maintenance program.** Schedule of all repair, inspection, cleaning, lubrication, and other tasks necessary to keep something in proper working order.

**management company.** Firm that specializes in Community Association management, hired by the Association to carry out the Board's policies and provide the day-to-day operation of the affairs of the Association.

**management letter.** Letter from an accountant or auditor with questions and suggestions regarding the financial aspects of managing the Association.

**management plan.** Program for operating the Community.

**manager.** Individual who specializes in Community Association management, hired by the Association to carry out the Board's policies and provide the day-to-day operation of the affairs of the Association.

**master deed.** Recorded instrument that describes the property involved in a Community Association and may contain specific references to properties in the Community Association subject to the master deed.

**mechanical maintenance.** Repair, inspection, lubrication, and cleaning of machines and tools, done to keep them in proper working condition.

**mediation.** Form of resolving disputes by using a neutral third party to assist in negotiation.

**meeting.** A gathering of association members, who discuss issues and make decisions on them through motions.

**minutes.** Official record of the proceedings of a meeting.

**motion.** Formal proposal, put before an assembly, on which action must be taken.

# N

**named insured.** Person or entity in an insurance policy entitled to indemnification by having a covered injury or liability.

**named peril insurance.** Policy under which only specified causes are considered to be covered.

**newsletter.** Printed periodical report devoted to news of and for the Association members and others associated with the Community.

# O

**operating budget.** Portion of the budget for the expenses of operating the Association, other than reserves.

**operating expenses.** Costs incurred to maintain a property and keep it productive.

**operating reserves.** Funds set aside for the payment of an annual expense.

**outside management.** Individual manager or management company whose representative does not live in the Community.

**owners manuals.** Manuals stating the policies and procedures of an Association that affect the members.

# P

**parliamentary procedure.** Established rules of parliamentary law and unwritten rules of courtesy used to facilitate the transaction of business in deliberative assemblies.

**payment schedule.** Plan for periodic payments for a debt or obligation, such as a stipulation for judgment.

**personal property.** Possessions that are temporary or movable, as opposed to real property, which is fixed.

**physical maintenance.** Repair, inspection, and cleaning of a physical facility to keep it in proper condition.

**planned community.** Community Association that is not a condominium, stock cooperative, or community apartment project.

**planned development.** Development having one or both of two features: first, a common area; and second, an Association with the power to assess a separate interest owner, such as a unit or apartment, and to lien such owner's interest. It is not necessarily one of the other three forms of CID.

**planned expenses.** Expenditures that are expected and intentionally provided for.

**pleading.** Written document filed in an action that seeks relief or sets out the reasons why no relief should be granted.

**premium.** Compensation to an insurer for accepting the risk of loss; cost of insurance.

**president of the board.** Elected officer responsible for the strategy and management of the Association.

**preventive maintenance.** Program of inspection and regular care that allows potential problems to be detected, and either solved early or prevented altogether.

**professional community association manager (PCAM).** The professional designation conferred by the Community Associations Institute on individuals who have met certain minimum levels of experience, education, and participation in the profession of Association management.

**property insurance.** Protection of an insured person's real or personal property against loss or damage.

**property tax.** Fee levied by local governments against real estate, business equipment, and inventories.

**project manager.** Individual employed by a management company with specific responsibility to oversee and manage a particular Community.

**proxy.** Authorization given to one person to vote in place of another.

# Q

**quorum.** Minimum number of members that must be present or votes that must be represented in person or by proxy at a meeting in order for business to be transacted legally.

# R

**real estate.** Land and all permanent improvements on it; realty.

**recess.** Short break in a business meeting.

**replacement cost.** Amount of money required to repair and replace an existing property with property of the same material and construction without deducting for depreciation.

**replacement reserves.** Funds set aside for probable repair and replacement of common area components at some future time.

**reserve study.** Document prepared every three years by the Association showing the physical condition of the property that it is obligated to monitor, the funds allocated for its upkeep and maintenance, and the planned annual use of those funds.

**reserves.** Funds set aside for special purposes; specifically, to enable an Association to meet nonrecurring and major expenses.

**resident handbook.** Book or manual setting out the basic rules and customs of the Association, as well as useful information about the general Community.

**resident manager.** Person who lives in the Community and acts as manager.

**resident referendum.** Vote by membership on fundamental changes in the CC&Rs or to recall a member of the Board.

**retainer.** Fee paid to a professional, such as a lawyer, in advance for future services.

**revenues.** Income accrued through any source that benefits the Association.

**risk.** Chance of a loss from a hazard.

**risk management.** Proactive and preventive systems designed to identify, address, or avoid future problems.

**Robert's Rules of Order.** Recognized formal guidelines for conducting a business meeting.

# S

**secretary of the board.** Elected officer on the Board of Directors responsible for all Association documentation and records.

**self-management.** Plan of running a Community whereby unit owners carry out policy decisions of and handle affairs for an Association; also called self-management structure.

**signatories.** People who are given the responsibility to sign documents.

**single family home.** Detached dwelling designed for occupancy by one family.

**special assessment.** Fee levied against unit owners to cover unexpected expenses.

**special meeting.** Unscheduled meeting called by the Board or membership to discuss urgent business.

**standing committee.** Group of people formed to handle ongoing business on a certain subject.

**statement of income and expense.** Financial report that indicates how much income has been earned and what expenses have been incurred over a certain period of time; also compares budgeted and actual figures for the period in question and year to date.

**stipulation for judgment.** Settlement procedure in which a judgment is signed by agreement, but not filed as long as an agreed series of periodic payments is paid in full. If there is a default as to a payment, the judgment may be entered by the court for the full stipulated amount, less payments made. If the agreed amount is timely paid, a dismissal is filed and there is no judgment recorded. Therefore, no negative public record is made.

**stock cooperative.** Development in which a corporation has title to the real property and the owners of the corporation have a right of exclusive occupancy of a portion of that real estate, along with their ownership of stock in the corporation.

**summary trial.** Abbreviated trial where many factual and legal issues are stipulated to by the parties, and only essential issues are decided by a jury, judge, or arbitrator.

# T

**taxable income.** The portion of revenue that is subject to taxation.

**tax exemption.** Freedom from liability on taxes that apply to others.

**tenant-in-common ownership.** Undivided interest in common with the other owners in a portion of real property known as the common areas of the project or development, which are separate and distinct from the separate interest areas, such as a unit or apartment.

**title.** Ownership of property and also the instrument that is evidence of that ownership.

**title insurance.** Contract that indemnifies a person against loss or damage from a defect in title to real property.

**treasurer of the board.** Elected officer on the Board of Directors responsible for all financial oversight and strategy for the Association.

# U

**user fees.** Fees collected for the use of facilities, such as extra parking or storage spaces, and other similar charges.

**utilities.** Community services rendered by public utility companies, such as gas, electricity, and telephone.

# V

**vice president of the board.** Elected officer who fulfills the President's responsibilities in his or her absence, and generally oversees the work of Committees.

# W

**waiver.** Surrender of a right or privilege.

**workers' compensation.** Provision, required by state law, to cover cost of medical care and weekly income payments to injured workers or their dependents for industrial injuries or diseases, regardless of blame.

**written stipulation.** Written agreement between people, commonly found in litigation.

# Z

**zoning commission.** Governmental body charged with the responsibility of enforcing or modifying zoning restrictions.

# –Appendix A–

# KEY QUESTIONS AND EVALUATIONS OF YOUR ASSOCIATION

From the moment you begin asking questions or evaluating your Association, you should understand that you are not asking about any particular person's performance. You are beginning to assess how the business of your Community works.

This makes the process of asking questions much easier for everyone involved. The questions are not personal. In asking them, they should not be turned into anything personal or be used to attack the person being questioned. The questions are simply questions. They are your means of identifying how to make your Community and its Association better.

As you begin collecting answers to the questions, if you find that information is not readily available or clear to you, you have just identified unnecessary complications in the Association and how it does business. The answers to the questions listed should always be immediately available. It is only upon seeing those answers that you can begin determining what needs to be done.

Do not let anyone tell you that you just do not understand. Granted, some issues are more technical than others, but that does not mean that you cannot understand. It just means that you need further explanation. As a business owner, it is your responsibility to understand what is going on in your Community. You have to protect your investment.

Look for answers, and while you are looking, check out how difficult it is to find those answers. If it is difficult, become involved. Work with those who are working on the difficult project or issue, and find out more about what they are doing and why. Discuss how the information can be made more readily available and easy to understand for all residents.

Complexity is not a problem. It is an opportunity. Wherever you find something you do not or cannot understand, you have found an opportunity to improve how your business operates. As a business owner, that is one of your goals—to make things make sense so that everyone benefits.

# THE BOARD QUESTIONS

### General Questions
- How many members are on the Board of Directors?
- How often are elections held?
- How many Board members are affected at each election?
- What is the impact of the election schedule for the Board? How does the schedule affect the running of the Association and its projects?
- What are the responsibilities of the Board as described by the governing documents?
- How well does the Board do in fulfilling those responsibilities as defined?
- Are there changes that should be made to the governing documents so that the Board can operate more efficiently and effectively in support of the Association?
- In which areas might the Board improve its performance as defined by the governing documents?
- Who are the officers on the Board?
- How are their positions defined?
- What specific roles or support do the officers provide to the Board and to the Community?

### Operational Questions
- Are written minutes taken at each meeting and made available to homeowners?
- Is the performance of the manager or management company and any contractors evaluated annually?
- Is it the Board's policy to regularly audit the important functions of the Association, such as financial, management, insurance, and vendor issues?

◆ Are Board members covered by Directors and Officers (D&O) insurance coverage in case of liability?

◆ What has the Association done to involve itself in local government and neighborhood groups to help influence a higher quality of life for the Community?

### Committee Questions

◆ Are the Committees directed by the Board and do they report at Board meetings in writing?

◆ How many Committees exist in the Association?
  ◆ Which are Standing Committees?
  ◆ Which are Ad Hoc?

◆ How many members serve on each Committee?

◆ What do the Committees do?

◆ Who is responsible for overseeing their activities?

◆ How do the Committees report on their findings and to whom do they report?

◆ Do Committees make decisions on their own or do they bring recommendations to the Board?

◆ How do the members of the Board interact with the Committee members?

◆ How are members of the Community made aware of Committee membership opportunities? How often do new members join the Committees?

# THE MANAGEMENT QUESTIONS

### General Questions

◆ How is the Association currently managed?

◆ Which of the management duties are performed by outside resources?

◆ What types of problems have there been either in the management of the Association or in the relationship between the manager and the Board?

◆ How might those problems be better addressed?

◆ Given the size and complexity of the Community, is it being managed by the appropriate resource?

◆ Do the services currently received from outside resources match those recommended? Should they?

◆ What improvements to the management of the Association might be recommended?

*Operational Questions*
- Are Association documents easily accessible to homeowners?
- Does management provide the proper agendas for regularly scheduled meetings as well as for the annual meeting?
- Are annual meeting minutes finalized within two weeks following the meeting?
- Does the Association have vendor contract bidding guidelines with at least three bids for review for items over a certain amount?
- Does the Association have up-to-date preventive maintenance manuals?

# RULES AND REGULATIONS QUESTIONS

- How are the rules and regulations of the Association established and communicated?
- How often does the Association review the rules and regulations for necessary updates and changes?
- Are the rules and regulations of the Association enforced consistently?
- How can we improve the rules and regulations and their enforcement, timeliness, and applicability to the Community?

# THE LEGAL QUESTIONS

*General Questions*
- Do you have a lawyer representing the Association with special expertise in Community Association law?
- Have the CC&Rs been reviewed recently? Are they up to date with legal statutes?
- How does the Board handle circumstances when Board members have a conflict of interest?
- What are the due process procedures for Association rule enforcement?
- Is there any litigation pending or anticipated?

*Legal Counsel Questions*
- What experience do you and your firm have representing Community Associations?
- What experience do you and your firm have handling the specific legal matter confronting our Association?

- As a Community Association lawyer, what types of services would you provide?
- Do you have other affiliations—other Associations, management companies, vendors, developers, or professional associations—within the Community Association industry?
- How is your firm organized in terms of delegation of responsibility for our Association's legal work?
- Does your firm have a policy regarding returning telephone calls? What is it?
- If necessary, are you prepared and qualified to represent our Association in a court of law?
- Have you or your firm had any malpractice claims made against you? Are you covered by malpractice insurance?
- What is your billing policy, including rates for you and others in your firm, billable time increments, retainers, billing frequency, and itemization of costs?
- What are some of the ways for our Association to reduce our legal costs?
- Can you provide us with references from current and former Association clients?
- Are there any questions you would like to ask us?

# THE FINANCE QUESTIONS

### General Questions
- Do you have an outside, objective CPA perform an annual audit of Association finances?
- Does the Treasurer of the Board, as well as the manager or management company, understand all the expenses and income well enough to explain them to homeowners each month if necessary?
- Who develops the budget? When is the budget distributed to the homeowners?
- Are collection policy procedures in place and published for the owners?
- Does the Association have adequate general liability and property insurance?

# ASSESSMENTS AND RESERVES QUESTIONS

- How often are assessments paid by homeowners?
- How are those assessments being used?
- How often and for what purpose have special assessments been paid?
- Are there any special assessments planned for the Association?
- What are the Community's regular, known expenses?
- Are those expenses justifiable?
- How much does the Association have in reserves? What percentage of the reserve funds are funded?
- What is planned for the use of those reserves and when?
- Given what is planned, is there enough?
- How are the reserves invested?
- Who is responsible for overseeing the investment of the reserve funds?
- Is there a contingency reserve account?

# REPAIR AND MAINTENANCE QUESTIONS

- Is it clear to all homeowners exactly what the common property of the Community is?
- How well maintained are the common areas?
- What types of repair and maintenance schedules exist?
- How responsive is the Association when a repair or maintenance request is submitted?
- What is the proper procedure—if there is one—for submitting repair or maintenance requests?

# –Appendix B–

# BOARD MEMBER
# ORIENTATION MANUAL

Whenever a new Board of Directors is established, you will be well served if you have an orientation program. It does not matter if some—or even all—of the Board members have held their offices before. The purpose of the orientation is to create an equal playing field for all Board members.

Serving on the Board does not have to be a painful or difficult experience. As long as you remember that you are there in support of the business of the Community—the Association—and not representing your own or anyone else's agenda, Board membership becomes an enjoyable experience.

Part of what makes it and keeps it enjoyable is having a clear understanding of the role of the Board, its responsibilities, how it functions, and what the support mechanisms are to ensure success. All of these are included in the orientation manual.

The suggested text for the manual can be adapted by you and your Community Association. Included here are the recommended basic components, but that does not mean that it has to be used in exactly this form for your Community. You should read it, take into consideration the specific needs of your Community and its Association, think about the various parts of the book that you thought particularly applied to your situation, and then customize the orientation manual to your needs.

You will notice that the manual text is written in a more formal and serious tone than much of the rest of this book. This is done on purpose. Board members must realize that they are important and that they are doing an important job.

Finally, it is recommended that you hold a special session for the Board members to discuss the orientation manual and its contents. At this meeting, the Board members will have the opportunity to raise any questions or issues they have as a result of the orientation manual. This provides Board members the opportunity not only to clarify the contents of the orientation manual, but also to better understand and clarify their role and responsibility as Board members.

The meeting should be scheduled within a month of giving the Board members the manual. This will ensure that any issues that might exist are identified and addressed quickly and cleanly, before they grow into problems and obstacles for the Board, the Association, and the Community.

# FROM THE PRESIDENT OF THE BOARD

[Begin with a letter from the President both welcoming the Board and addressing its importance to the Community. The text might read as follows.]

Welcome.

As a member of the Board of Directors of our Association, you have taken on an important and challenging role—to assist in ensuring the ongoing success and welfare of our Community. Your insight, experience, and active participation will play a vital role in the safety and success of our Association and our Community as a whole.

The Board of Directors is entrusted with maintaining and improving our quality of living. We are the means by which owners— including ourselves—increase the value and quality of our property. We protect our Community and each individual's investment in that Community through our work. We assist in creating the highest and finest quality of life for our Community. We protect the Community and all of its inhabitants now and in the future through the thoughtfulness and integrity of the decisions we make.

The Board of Directors is responsible for managing the business of the Community. As a member of the Board, you will be called upon to make difficult and sometimes unpopular decisions regarding the Community. Your responsibility is to the Community as a whole. This includes all homeowners—not just those you know or those who present you with their thoughts and feelings.

As a member of the Board of Directors, you are a leader in the Community. Your contribution will be great and greatly appreciated. We all look forward to a successful year and the opportunity to gain from your participation.

Sincerely,

President

[The manual should move immediately into the operational responsibilities of the Board. The following sections provide suggested text discussing the areas on which the Board will focus in the upcoming year.]

# PURPOSE OF THE BOARD

The primary purpose of the Board of Directors is to protect, preserve, and enhance the value of the property. In our Community and as a part of the ongoing operations of our Association, we are in the enviable position of not having to start from scratch.

Instead, our charter as the Board of Directors is to continue the good work pursued by previous Boards. It is our responsibility to bring our own creative thought to enhancing, augmenting, and growing the Community even further.

The following describes areas and issues on which the Board must focus. These focus areas are by no means comprehensive. As we work together throughout the year we will add components leading to a better Community, a better-managed Association and an even more thorough orientation for our successors.

By focusing on these areas, we are working to achieve our primary purpose—both now and for the future.

## PROGRESS TO DATE

At the beginning of each year, all Board Members will be provided with a progress review for the past one to three years. This review will include, but not be limited to, information on the financial status of the Association, current and planned activities and expenses, and Committee activities and oversight. Issues and concerns from Committees and throughout the Community will be presented for discussion and consideration.

Members of the Community will be provided with a summary of the past year's progress, as well as outstanding and ongoing issues and activities. This information will be provided in the first Community Newsletter published each year.

## PLANNING FOR THE FUTURE

Each year, the Board of Directors will establish a clear set of goals for the Board and for the Community. Specific assignments associated with the goals will be made and a progress review will occur at each Board meeting. These goals will be published to the Community. Where applicable, Committee participation in the achievement of the goals will be assigned.

Members of the Board and management must be as current as possible on larger Community issues. In order to ensure the highest possible knowledge base, Board members and management should participate in local and, if appropriate, national Community Association Institute (CAI) activities. This will assist Board members and management in fulfilling their purpose and goals for the Community.

# FINANCIAL MANAGEMENT

An annual audit will be conducted by an outside CPA firm. Results will be presented to the Board for review, discussion, and further action.

A reserve study should be conducted every three years. At that time, determinations should be made regarding future reserve needs for expected and unplanned expenses.

An annual vendor review will be pursued. The purpose of this review is to determine the quality and value of the work being provided by current vendors, as well as to open opportunities for other vendors to support the Community. The review will be overseen by the manager, and the results will be presented to the Board for review and further action.

# COMMUNITY OPERATIONS

Notices for Board and Committee meetings will be posted at least four days in advance of the meeting. The notice should include the time, date, location, and agenda for the meeting.

Committees will submit recommendations to the Board for consideration and approval. Expenses associated with each recommendation must be submitted in detail. At the time of approval and before spending any monies, the Board should determine as precisely as possible where the monies can reasonably come from. Once that determination is made and approval is given, action towards the recommendation can be taken.

# BOARD OPERATIONS

Executive sessions of the Board of Directors are to be called only to discuss those matters that either cannot or should not be discussed publicly for legal reasons or for the protection of the Community and the Board. Examples of issues appropriate for an executive session are the terms and nature of contracts, employment matters, legal problems, and disciplinary actions against members. Requests for an executive session should be submitted to the President of the Board at least one week in advance of the next scheduled Board meeting.

Each member of the Board of Directors should serve on a Committee. Assignments of Board members to Committees will be made during the first Board meeting of each year. This will allow Board members to act as liaisons with the Committees, and more importantly, to enhance the sense of participation and community between Board members and the Community.

# BOARD CONDUCT

The Board sets the tone for the Community. As such, members must behave respectfully and appropriately toward one another. By doing so, they act as positive role models for the other homeowners. As elected leaders of the Community Association, the Board is responsible for establishing and maintaining the sense of community. This is most directly and easily accomplished by consistently demonstrating and modeling the types of behaviors that must be the norm throughout the Community.

[The following suggested text conveys that appropriate behavior and its importance.]

## Rules of Conduct

- Comments presented to and by the Board about issues and concerns should address the issue or concern only. Personal comments or attacks are neither necessary nor acceptable.
- Whenever possible, issues between Community members should be resolved by those members on a one-on-one basis. The Board is responsible for the overall operations of the Community—not the resolution of individual differences. Only cases in which a member of the Community is violating Association rules or regulations should the Board become involved.
- Rules established for the Community—homeowners and renters alike—should be reasonable, positive, and enforced consistently across the Community. A well-informed Community with consistently enforced rules harbors fewer ill feelings, leading to fewer counterproductive actions.
- Renters should be treated as homeowners are treated. While not having the same direct financial investment as homeowners, renters are a part of the human community.
- Avoid any individual or hidden agendas of your own or from the Community members. These agendas, no matter how well intentioned, are counterproductive to the workings of the Board and to the Community as a whole.

# COMMITTEE DESCRIPTIONS

The following text introduces the five Standing Committees recommended. These Committees are Architectural, Legal, Financial, Communications, and Social. Each Board member should serve on a Committee both to support the Committee and to act as liaison with the Board.

The primary purpose of the Board-approved Committees is to provide guidance to the Board of Directors. This is accomplished through the research, recommendations, actions, and monitoring performed by each Committee within its charter. The Committees also act as a conduit and liaison between the larger Community population and the Board. This ensures that the decisions made and actions taken are known to and supported by the members of the Community.

Ad Hoc Committees can be established by the Board at the request of Community or Board members by petitioning the Board during a regularly scheduled Board meeting. At the time that such Committees might be established, the purpose and charter of the Committee, as well as its expected output and timelines, will be determined. A Board member will be assigned to that Ad Hoc Committee to act as a liaison.

## Architectural Committee

The Architectural Committee provides guidance to the Board regarding the architectural needs and standards for the Community. These include but are not limited to the preservation, safety, and enhancement of the physical environment, as well as the procedures for submission, review, and approval of architectural plans. Of great importance is the Committee's tracking and monitoring of the enforcement of architectural standards and Board-approved projects that are underway. The Committee works with the manager to develop and implement programs that promote the safety and security of the Community.

## Legal Committee

The Legal Committee provides guidance to the Board through its review and recommendation of rules and regulations related to Community, Association, and Board operations. This includes, but is not limited to, a review of rules and rule enforcement, amicable settlement procedures for possible rule violations, updates and changes to the governing documents, and the tracking and monitoring of consistent enforcement procedures. The Committee is also responsible for the review of insurance policies and claims history. Recommendations from this Committee include the ways by which real and potential legal and financial risk can be reduced.

## Financial Committee

The Financial Committee provides guidance to the Board through its ongoing review of the financial status of the Community, as well as its recommendations regarding means of improving that financial position. This is accomplished through the Committee's proposed annual budgets and monitoring of Association finances. Monitoring activities include, but are not limited to, scheduling and oversight of outside audits, reserve reviews, and vendor reviews, as well as project finance tracking and proposed budget justification. This Committee provides support to other Committees and the manager when projects requiring financial expenditure are being proposed. In such cases, the Financial Committee is also responsible for recommending the source of funding for the proposed project.

## Communications Committee

The Communications Committee is the primary liaison between the Board, the Committees, and the Community. The Committee is responsible for all the means by which the Community is kept apprised of Board- and Association-approved activities. Newsletters, notices, calls for input by the Board and Committees, and so on are designed, implemented, managed, and monitored by this Committee. In providing guidance to the Board, the Committee is responsible for recommending improvements to the ways by which information is disseminated to the Community and received by the Board and Committees, including follow-up mechanisms and Community response.

## Social Committee

The Social Committee is responsible for setting the tone and fostering the sense of community enjoyed by all of the residents of the Community. The Committee recommends, oversees, and reviews Community-sponsored activities, social programs, new member welcome, etc. Working with the Communications Committee, this Committee ensures that all Community members are informed of upcoming events and activities well in advance. In providing guidance to the Board, the Committee is responsible for recommending means of expanding the sense of and participation by the Community.

# CONCLUSION

The purpose of this manual is to give you as a Board Member an overview of the general duties of the Board and of its individual members.

Again, welcome to the Board.

# –Appendix C–

# RECOMMENDED READINGS AND RESOURCES

The variety of books, magazines, special reports, and resources specifically addressing Community and Homeowners Associations is overwhelming. There are some core resources, however, that will allow you to better understand the specifics of the Association.

Some of these are books and are practically timeless. Others are magazines and reports that provide an ongoing update on all the things homeowners should be aware of. Finally, there are those organizational resources that provide ever-expanding information and service to the homeowner and manager.

Do not limit your reading to only the specific type of Community or the state in which you live. While certain aspects of the law, statutes, or regulations might be Community- or location-specific, the majority of the information offered in these resources will provide you with valuable information and guidance.

## BOOKS

Bickel, Branden E. and D. Andrew Sirkin. *The Condominium Bluebook*. Piedmont Press, 2006

Bramson, Robert M., PhD. *Coping With Difficult People*. Dell Publishing, 1988

Canfield, Jack. *The Successful Principles: How to Get from Where You Are to Where You Want to Be*. Harper Collins, 2005

Cava, Roberta. *Dealing with Difficult People, How to Deal with Nasty Customers, Demanding Bosses and Annoying Co-workers*. Firefly Books, 2004

Dwoskin, Hale. *The Sedona Method: Your Key to Lasting Happiness, Success, Peace, and Emotional Well Being.* Sedona Press, 2003

Grimm, Beth A. and Jim R. Lane. *Finding the Key to Your Castle, A Guide to Cooperative Living in Your Condominium, Townhouse or Planned Development Home.* Grimm-Lane, 1995

Hanna, John Paul and Grace Morioka. *Homeowners Associations: A How-to Guide for Leadership and Effective Participation.* Hanna Press, 1999

Hickenbottom, Jan. *Questions & Answers about Community Associations.* Miller Publishing, 2002

Institute of Real Estate Management. *The Owner's and Manager's Guide to Condominium Management, Revised Edition.* National Association of Realtors, 1994

Keatts, M.J., editor, *Conducting Meetings: A Guide to Running Productive Community Association Board Meetings,* Community Associations Institute, 1998

Stephens, Joyce L. *Guide for the Presiding Officer: A Functional Guide for Presidents and Chairmen, Third Edition.* Frederick Publishers, 2000

# MAGAZINES AND SPECIAL REPORTS

*The California Homeowners Association Legal Digest,* bi-monthly newsletter, by subscription from www.californiacondoguru.com

*Common Ground,* CAI's magazine for condominium and homeowner associations

*CondoManagement Magazine,* www.condomgmt.com

*Guide for Association Practitioners (GAP) Report Series,* Community Associations Institute (CAI)

State of California, Department of Real Estate, "Living in a California Common Interest Development," August 2002, www.dre.cahwnet.gov/cidinfo.htm

# RESOURCES

**Building Owners and Managers Institute (BOMI)**
1521 Ritchie Highway
Arnold, MD 21012
800-235-2664
410-974-1410
Fax: 410-974-0544
www.bomi-edu.org

**California Association of Community Managers (CACM)**
23461 South Pointe Drive
Suite 200
Laguna Hills, CA 92653
949-916-2226
Toll-Free in Northern CA:
  800-363-9771
Fax: 949-916-5557
www.cacm.org

**Community Associations Institute (CAI)**
National Chapter
225 Reinekers Lane
Suite 300
Alexandria, VA 22314
703-548-8600
Toll-Free Member Line:
  888-224-4321
Fax: 703-684-1581
www.caionline.org

**Executive Council of Homeowners (ECHO)**
1602 The Alameda
Suite 101
San Jose, CA 95126
408-297-3246
Fax: 408-297-3517
www.echo-ca.org

**Foundation for Community Association Research**
225 Reinekers Lane
Suite 300
Alexandria, VA 22314
703-548-8600
Fax: 703-684-1581
www.cairf.org

**HOA Document Review**
331 Pierce Road
San Jose, CA 95138
408-226-2437
866-462-3627
Fax: 408-351-4307
www.hoadocumentreview.com

**HOA Yellow Pages**
1611 Telegraph Avenue
Suite 1450
Oakland, CA 94612
510-465-2073
Fax: 510-465-7035
www.hoayellowpages.com

**Institute of Real Estate Management (IREM)**
430 North Michigan Avenue
Chicago, IL 60611
800-837-0706
Fax: 800-338-4736
www.irem.org

**National Association For Community Mediation**
1527 New Hampshire Avenue, NW
Washington, DC 20036
202-667-9700
Fax: 202-667-8629
www.nafcm.org

**National Association of Housing
Cooperatives**
1707 H Street, NW
Suite 201
Washington, DC 20006
202-737-0797
Fax: 202-783-7869
www.coophousing.org

**National Association of Realtors**
430 North Michigan Avenue
Chicago, IL 60611
800-874-6500
Fax: 312-329-5960
www.realtor.org

**The National Board of Certification
  for Community Association
  Managers (NBC-CAM)**
225 Reinekers Lane
Suite 310
Alexandria, VA 22314
703-836-6902
Fax: 703-837-9490
www.nbccam.org

**U.S. Department of Housing &
  Urban Development (HUD)**
451 7th Street, SW
Washington, DC 20410
202-708-1112
www.hud.gov

**U.S. Department of Labor**
Bureau of Labor Statistics
(see especially Property, Real Estate,
  and Community Association
  Managers)
www.bls.gov

# INDEX

# Q

quorum, 162, 164, 166, 196

# R

real estate, 12, 190, 196, 197
recommendations, 19, 22, 24, 27,
  29, 30, 31, 33, 38, 40, 42, 59,
  127, 130, 137, 138, 140, 146,
  149, 150, 154, 158, 162
recordkeeping, 37, 146, 147
records, 24, 25, 52, 80, 83, 125,
  147, 188, 197
relationships, 3, 32, 38, 39, 40,
  41, 46, 47, 49, 52, 62, 65, 108,
  144, 145, 179, 191, 192
repairs, 9, 10, 11, 110, 117, 122,
  125, 126, 127, 128, 137, 138,
  147, 148, 190, 194, 195, 196
reserves, 9, 12, 13, 14, 15, 23, 26,
  30, 47, 51, 112, 124, 125, 126,
  127, 128, 129, 130, 135, 137,
  138, 158, 166, 171, 190, 195,
  196
residents, 3, 4, 5, 6, 8, 9, 10, 12,
  15, 16, 17, 20, 21, 22, 24, 27,
  31, 33, 34, 38, 42, 51, 82, 94,
  95, 96, 97, 98, 99, 102, 103,
  104, 108, 110, 111, 113, 114,
  115, 116, 117, 118, 139, 140,
  141, 142, 143, 169, 171, 172,
  173, 175, 177, 184, 196
responsibilities, 1, 3, 4, 6, 7, 8–9,
  11, 13, 15, 17, 19, 20, 21, 22,
  23, 24, 25, 26, 28, 31, 32, 33,
  34, 37, 38, 43, 44, 52, 61, 62,
  94, 95, 96, 97, 98, 110, 116,
  145, 158, 169, 177, 184, 185,
  191, 193, 196, 197, 198
retainers, 40, 43, 123, 196
revenues, 12, 125, 126, 127, 144,
  189, 191, 197, 198
risk management, 7, 14, 15, 23,
  30, 40, 41, 54, 60, 101, 108,
  122, 129, 130, 137, 138, 155,
  187, 192, 195, 197
Robert's Rules of Order, 58, 59,
  197
Rules and Regulations, 8, 9, 10,
  15, 16, 17, 18, 23, 29, 100,
  157, 169, 171
  enforcement, 16, 17, 18, 29,
    41, 50, 53, 58, 59, 60, 61,
    65, 70, 80, 94, 98, 99, 116,
    142, 169, 191

# S

safety, 1, 2, 29, 33, 39, 41, 95,
  125, 129, 136, 139, 145, 179
salary, 37, 126
schools, 54, 140, 179
Secretary, 23, 25, 52, 101, 150,
  154, 160, 164, 197
security, 13, 29, 33, 34, 59, 70,
  82, 90, 136, 141, 142, 143,
  164, 170, 171
services, 4, 7, 9, 10, 12, 16, 23,
  34, 35, 36, 37, 38, 42, 90, 113,
  115, 129, 136, 137, 140, 144,
  170, 171, 172, 177, 179, 188,
  192, 193, 196, 198
shareholders, 44, 190
shelter in place, 140

# ABOUT THE AUTHORS

**Dr. Marlene M. Coleman** has lived in a condominium community in Los Angeles for the past twenty-five years. She has held positions as a Committee and Board member, as well as served two terms as President of the Board of her Community Association—having turned it around from near disaster. She is also actively involved in both state and national Community Association organizations. Dr. Coleman is Associate Clinical Professor of Family Medicine at the University of Southern California Medical School and an Attending Physician in College Health at the California Institute of Technology in Pasadena, California. She is a ten-year top executive in a medical liability protection company. Dr. Coleman is also the author of *Safe and Sound: Healthy Travel with Children* (Globe Pequot Press, 2003) and *Start Your Own Medical Practice* (Sphinx Publishing, 2006).

**Judge William Huss** is a full-time mediator and arbitrator, overseeing individual, institutional, and corporate cases, and he was named one of the Master Mediators by Verdict Magazine. Judge Huss retired from the Los Angeles Superior Court after presiding over both civil and criminal trials. He also served on the Los Angeles Superior Court Executive Committee and was the Chair of the Education Subcommittee. He is the cofounder and five-year President of a mediation and arbitration company. Judge Huss has been a Board Member and President of his Community Association, served on the Legal Committee for over twenty years—sixteen of them as Chairman—and is an associate member of the California Association of Community Managers. Judge Huss is the author of *Start Your Own Law Practice* (Sphinx Publishing, 2005) and is completing *Shake On It*, a book on negotiation and mediation.